FUTURE-PROOFING YOUR SIL BUSINESS

COMPILED BY TANIA GOMEZ

*Turtle*Publishing

Copyright © 2025 Tania Gomez

All rights reserved. No part of this publication may be reproduced, stored in a retrieval system, or transmitted in any form or by any means, electronic, mechanical, photocopying, recording or otherwise, without prior written permission of the author.

Legal Notice: This book is copyright protected. This book is only for personal use. You cannot amend, distribute, sell, use, quote or paraphrase any part, or the content within this book, without the consent of the author or publisher.

Disclaimer: Please note the information contained within this document is for educational and entertainment purposes only. All effort has been executed to present accurate, up to date, and reliable, complete information. No warranties of any kind are declared or implied. Readers acknowledge that the authors are not engaging in the rendering of legal, financial, medical or professional advice. The content within this book has been derived from various sources. Please consult a licensed professional before attempting any techniques outlined in this book.

By reading this document, the reader agrees that under no circumstances is the author responsible for any losses, direct or indirect, which are incurred as a result of the use of the information contained within this document, including, but not limited to — errors, omissions, or inaccuracies.

Published by Turtle Publishing
Cover & Interior Design by Kathy Shanks

ISBN: 978-1-7643960-4-2 (paperback)
ISBN: 978-1-7643960-5-9 (ebook)

turtlepublishing.com.au

To my SIL clients,

You show up every single day, in a system that doesn't always make it easy, and still you give your best. You care deeply, serve fully, and keep going, rain, hail or shine. I'm constantly in awe of your grit, your heart, and your drive to serve.

As Gandhi said, "The best way to find yourself is to lose yourself in the service of others." You live this every day, and it's a privilege to walk beside you.

TABLE OF CONTENTS

1 Introduction
- 2   How This Book Works
- 5   Why This Book Matters Now
- 6   Let's Keep Going

PART 1
HOME IS WHERE THE HEART IS

9 Healthy Homes
By Scott Chapman
- 10   What Makes a Healthy Home?
- 11   The Power of Small Environmental Changes
- 13   Support Workers as Gateways to Wellness
- 15   The Economic Case for Healthier Homes
- 17   Reframing Choice and Control
- 19   Innovation in Practice
- 21   Action Steps for Providers
- 22   Scott's SIL Health Kickstart Plan
- 23   Final Wrap-Up, The Future We're Building Towards

25 Getting Complex Care Right
By Caroline Yates
- 26   What is Complex Care?
- 28   Redefining Complex Care in Disability Housing

30 Creating Calm, Making Complex Care Feel Like Home
32 What Providers Get Wrong
35 Building a Network Around the Work
37 The Future of Complex Care in SIL

41 Meeting the Participant Where They're At
By Luke Wilson

42 Meeting People Where They're At
45 Honouring Pace and Building Trust
47 Empathy Over Expertise
49 Systems Without Losing Soul
51 Balancing Risk, Autonomy, and Accountability
53 A Future Led by Participants
54 The Practice of Co-Design

57 What Good Supports Feel Like
By Ryan Simon

58 Being Put Somewhere That Wasn't Right for Me
60 The Moment I Felt Like I Mattered
61 What Good SIL Looks Like
62 My Future and Yours
63 Being Real is the Support

PART 2
THE PULSE OF THE PRACTICE

67 **Building Strong Frontline Leadership**
By Dave Wells

- 68 Why Frontline Leadership Makes or Breaks an SIL Home
- 70 Skills That Matter
- 72 Systems That Set Leaders Up to Succeed
- 74 Culture, Retention, and Growth
- 75 Real Advice for SIL Providers
- 77 The Future of SIL Leadership
- 79 Learning Leadership the Hard Way

81 **Claiming and Its Impact on the Bottom Line**
By Josh Pix

- 82 Claiming as a Strategic Priority
- 84 Common Gaps and Risks
- 86 Building the Right Systems
- 88 Financial Sustainability and Future-Proofing
- 89 The Future of Claiming
- 91 Why Claiming Is Everyone's Business

93 Building Teams That Stay
By Charlene Woodbine

- 94 Why Training Matters for Retention
- 97 Designing Training That Works
- 99 Section 3: Culture, Growth, and Engagement
- 101 Retention and Long-Term Impact
- 104 Practical Roadmap for SIL Providers
- 106 The Bigger Picture

109 Setting a Strong Foundation with Quality Processes
By Tania Gomez

- 110 Why Quality Matters in SIL
- 113 What Quality Looks Like in SIL Homes
- 116 Culture, Environment, and Audit Readiness
- 120 Final Takeaways

PART 3
REIMAGINING INDEPENDENT FUTURES

125 Using Technology to Optimise Workflows
By Dr Heena Sinha Cheung

    126 Technology That Solves Real Problems
    127 Building the Right Tech Stack
    130 Getting Teams Onboard
    132 Future-Ready Operations
    135 Safety, Security, and Trust
    137 Be Brave, Start Small

139 Think Before You Act
By Chris Lapa

    140 Start with Strategy
    144 Section 2: Audience & Journey Mapping
    150 Digital Tools & Smart Tactics
    155 Section 4: Sales Process & Promotion
    158 Section 5: Partnerships, Referrals & Ecosystems
    161 Messaging, Brand & Storytelling
    164 Metrics, Data & Optimisation
    166 Long-Term Positioning & Growth
    169 Final Thought: The Strategy of Deep Thinking

173 Rethinking Participant Matching with Technology
By Aaron Cotton

- 178 The Future of Disability Housing
- 180 The SIL vs ILO Debate
- 181 Vanity Metrics
- 182 The Viability of Trust
- 183 It's About the People, Not the Properties
- 184 "Okay, Aaron, that's great, but how is this different from any of the other vacancy-filling sites?"
- 185 Conclusion

187 AI and the Future of Tech in Disability Support
By Sabeh Hassan

- 188 What AI Really Means for Disability Services
- 189 Saving Time Without Cutting Corners
- 191 Predictive, Not Reactive
- 193 Addressing Fear and Ethics
- 195 First Steps for SIL Providers
- 197 Foundations Before Features
- 199 Keeping Technology Person-Centred

203 CONCLUSION: Keep Going, Keep Building
By Tania Gomez

206 Keep Learning with Us
    206 The SILosophy Podcast
    206 The SIL Summit
    206 The Provider Collective
    207 Reach Out to the Authors
    207 Work with Me One-on-One

INTRODUCTION

By Tania Gomez

Over the last decade, most of the providers I've worked with have been in Supported Independent Living (SIL). And no matter how many audits I've done or businesses I've supported, the reality remains the same. SIL is hard, really hard.

It's messy. It's high risk. It's unpredictable. You're managing 24/7 rosters, staff who are burning out, participants with complex needs, tenancy issues, NDIS price changes, claiming rules, audits, behaviours of concern, and somehow, in the middle of all of that, you're expected to keep everyone safe, compliant, and thriving.

A good SIL provider can change the course of someone's life. A bad one can destroy it. I've seen both. And when SIL goes wrong, the consequences aren't just reputational or financial. They're personal. They're devastating. Because the people we support in SIL are often the most vulnerable and the least likely to be heard.

That's why I've always believed getting SIL right isn't about the business, it's about the quality of life for the person with disability living in this environment. Yet there's nothing out there that clearly shows SIL providers what good looks like. No guide. No strategy. No shared standard to hold onto.

I decided to help fill that gap. Three years ago, we launched the SIL Summit, and more than 1000 providers have joined us since. We created the SILosophy podcast to keep the conversation going.

What I've seen through all of it is that providers care. They want to do better, but most of them are doing it without real support, buried under red tape, and trying to lead in systems that weren't designed to help them succeed.

This book is a response to that. It's the lived knowledge of people working inside the chaos, providers, leaders, consultants, and advocates who've been where you are, and who've committed to doing it better.

How This Book Works

We've structured the book around three key parts. Each one reflects a layer of SIL service delivery, starting at the ground level with the experience of participants, moving through daily operations, and finishing with bold ideas about what SIL could look like in the future.

Part 1: Home is Where the Heart is

This section focuses on what it feels like to live in an SIL home. From safety and belonging to the nuance of complex care, it's about getting the human stuff right first.

- **Chapter 1. Healthy Homes, Scott Chapman**
  'SIL isn't just about support. It's about belonging.'
  Scott lays the groundwork with what every SIL provider needs to prioritise first, the home. He explains how to create safe, compliant environments that actually feel like home.

- **Chapter 2. Getting Complex Care Right, Caroline Yates**
  'Complexity isn't an excuse. It's a responsibility.'

Caroline unpacks the systems and clinical oversight needed to support participants with high needs safely and consistently.

- **Chapter 3. Meeting the Participant Where They're At, Luke Wilson**

  'Support that ignores context will always fall short.'

  Luke explains what individualised support really means, and how to make it part of your everyday delivery.

- **Chapter 4. What Good Supports Feel Like, Ryan Simmon**

  'People remember how you made them feel, not what your policy said.'

  Ryan brings the participant perspective, reminding us what safety, respect, and care look like from the inside out.

Part 2: The Pulse of the Practice

This section gets into the engine room of your service. Rosters, leadership, claims, staff retention, compliance. The unglamorous stuff that holds everything together.

- **Chapter 5. Building Strong Frontline Leadership, Dave Wells**

  'Frontline staff don't just need training. They need someone to believe in them.'

  Dave shows how strong team leaders build culture, manage risk, and hold everything together on the ground.

- **Chapter 6. Claiming and Its Impact on the Bottom Line, Josh Pix**

  'You can't run a quality service on broken cash flow.'

Josh explains how smart claiming processes protect your sustainability and avoid the panic cycles we see in SIL every day.

- **Chapter 7. Building Teams That Stay, Charlene Woodbine**
  'Retention isn't about perks. It's about purpose.'
  Charlene shares what really keeps staff in SIL and how to build teams that stick around and step up.
- **Chapter 8. Setting a Strong Foundation with Quality Processes, Tania Gomez**
  'Compliance is not about passing audits. It's about protecting people.'
  I break down what quality systems should look like and how to use them to lead with confidence, not fear.

Part 3: Reimagining Independent Futures

This section invites you to think bigger. It looks at how technology, data, and mindset shifts can help us build a more sustainable, future-ready version of SIL.

- **Chapter 9. Using Technology to Optimise Workflows, Heena**
  'Tech should reduce friction, not add to it.'
  Heena explores how the right systems can streamline your operations and give staff more time to focus on support.
- **Chapter 10. Think Before You Act, Chris Lapa**
  'Intentional action is the only kind worth taking.'
  Chris calls out knee-jerk decisions and shows how to plan better, grow strategically, and avoid costly mistakes.

- **Chapter 11. Rethinking Participant Matching with Technology, Aaron Cotton**
  'Getting the right match changes everything.'
  Aaron breaks down how tech can improve participant compatibility and reduce disruption and risk in homes.
- **Chapter 12. AI and the Future of Tech in Disability Support, Sabeh Hassan**
  'The future is not about replacing people. It's about supporting them better.'
  Sabeh walks through what AI might mean for our sector, and how we can prepare without losing our humanity.

Why This Book Matters Now

Supported Independent Living is one of the most important and under-supported parts of the NDIS. It's also one of the most exposed.

Providers are being pulled in every direction and are expected to manage risk, run sustainable businesses, support vulnerable people, and respond to an ever-changing system with little clear guidance.

There are constant updates, but rarely any clarity. There's pressure to improve, but no shared definition of what good actually looks like. There's no central space to learn from those who've done it before or done it better.

That's the gap this book fills.

It brings together the knowledge, experience, and ideas of people who have been where you are, providers, leaders, and advocates who have faced the same mess and found ways through it.

This isn't about theory or ticking boxes. It's about improving practice. It's about finding stability in the chaos, structure in the complexity, and purpose in the work.

We didn't write this book because we had all the answers. We wrote it because the sector deserves better questions, better tools, and better support.So if you're looking for a polished manual, you won't find it here. But if you're looking for insight that's practical, honest, and rooted in lived experience, you're holding it.

Let's Keep Going

To the authors, thank you for showing up with honesty, experience, and the willingness to share what most people keep behind closed doors. You've helped build something that will genuinely move the sector forward.

To the reader, thank you for being here. For carving out the time, for wanting to do better, and for staying open even when this work is exhausting.

This book was never about ticking boxes. It's about setting a new standard. Not through perfection, but through practice. Through community. Through people like you deciding that just surviving the system isn't enough.

If something in these pages challenges you, good. If something sparks an idea, even better. Take what's useful. Share it. Test it. Talk about it.

This is not the end of the conversation. It's an invitation to keep going together. We get better when we learn from each other. So stay connected. Reach out. Ask questions. Keep the momentum going. Because SIL is too important to leave to chance.

Tania Gomez

PART 1
HOME IS WHERE THE HEART IS

Creating safe, participant-first homes that feel like more than just accommodation.

'The ache for home lives in all of us. The safe place where we can go as we are and not be questioned.'
—Maya Angelou

CHAPTER 1
HEALTHY HOMES
BY SCOTT CHAPMAN

Scott Chapman is a multi-business owner and the co-founder of *Able Digital Wellness*, a preventative health platform transforming how people with disability experience care. Drawing on over a decade of experience building and scaling businesses, Scott has focused his energy on creating solutions that improve health, well-being, and independence for people with disability.

Able Digital Wellness was co-designed with allied health professionals and validated by Griffith University. The platform delivers tailored exercise, nutrition, and wellness programs alongside tools for support workers to track progress, communicate with families, and deliver more person-centred care.

Scott is passionate about using technology to create better outcomes for individuals and providers alike, helping to reduce negative behaviour incidents, increase healthy activity, and foster longer, healthier, and happier lives for people with disability.

• • •

CONNECT WITH SCOTT AT:
WEBSITE: abledigitalwellness.com.au
LINKED IN: @scott-chapman-abledigitalwellness

What Makes a Healthy Home?

When we talk about health in the NDIS space, most people go straight to clinical interventions. It's usually about funding for therapies, GP appointments, or allied health services, if they're lucky enough to access them. But for me, a healthy home starts well before any of that. It starts with the environment someone lives in. It's asking the question, 'Is this somewhere you'd be happy for your mum, your brother, or your own child to live?'

For a lot of people living in Supported Independent Living (SIL), what we call 'home' is just four walls and a roof. That's not a home. It's accommodation. And we've normalised that for too long.

I remember a conversation I had early on with a participant named Desh. He said to me, 'SIL and SDA are just glorified prisons.' That stuck with me. If you strip away all the things that make a space feel like it belongs to you, photos on the wall, a bit of greenery, the smell of your favourite meal, then you're not really supporting someone to live. You're managing them. And that's not what any of us got into this work to do.

To me, a healthy home enables choice and control, but not just for the sake of it. It has to lead to better outcomes. It's not only about exercise or food. It's about emotional well-being, social connection, and daily rhythms that feel familiar and meaningful. It's about creating a space where someone wants to get out of bed in the morning.

That looks different for every person. What feels homey to me might not feel homey to you. But some universal things matter. A healthy home doesn't feel clinical. It doesn't feel like a workplace. Sure, we've got to have things like sign-in books and compliance charts. That's part of our job. But it doesn't mean the walls need to be blank or the furniture needs to be beige. You can still have colour. You can still have family photos. You can still make space for a birthday banner or a footy scarf.

This is where I think the NDIS conversation around health often misses the mark. We spend so much time on what's funded, what's billable, or what's in someone's plan that we forget about the foundation. If the place someone comes home to every day feels institutional, then you've already made things harder than they need to be. You can't build wellbeing on top of a space that feels cold and impersonal.

I'm not talking about expensive renovations. Most of the time, it's the small details that make the biggest difference. The lighting. The smell of food cooking. A couch that feels lived in, not purchased in bulk. These are the things that create a connection to a place. They quietly communicate 'you belong here'.

If we truly want to support people to live better, it starts with the spaces they live in.

The Power of Small Environmental Changes

You don't need a brand-new build to improve someone's life. In fact, some of the most powerful changes I've seen in SIL environments have come from tiny adjustments: rearranging a kitchen, labelling drawers, making one room the go-to space for activities. These changes don't cost much, but they shift behaviour, improve wellbeing, and build community inside the home.

One of the best examples I've seen came from a house where the team decided to create a weekly 'cook together' night. All they did was declutter the kitchen, label a few key areas, and add a couple of shared utensils. That's it. Nothing fancy. But suddenly, everyone in the house started cooking together one night a week. The kitchen became a space for connection, not just function. It improved relationships, encouraged healthier food habits, and gave people something to look forward to.

In another house, we used what was already available, two living rooms. One became a dedicated activity room. We didn't gut it or fit it out with expensive gear. We just made it clear: this is the space for health and wellness. We left an iPad set up for accessing Able Digital Wellness content. We had a few resistance bands nearby. People knew that when they walked into that room, it was time to move, stretch, or try something new. It worked because it was consistent and intentional. It wasn't about design perfection. It was about purpose.

Too often, I see SIL homes that feel like a series of general-purpose rooms. There's no rhythm, no zoning, no cues that help someone understand what each part of the house is for. But when you create defined spaces, even just visually, you build confidence and routine. That could be as simple as a calming corner with soft colours and low lighting, or a breakout area where people can go if they need a moment alone. These elements are especially important for participants with sensory sensitivities.

The way we lay out a home can also impact how people relate to each other. Communal kitchens, open-plan dining areas, or even just moving a table to allow for more shared access can foster interaction and reduce isolation. You don't need a full design team to achieve that. You just need to be thoughtful about how people use and experience the space.

Small changes also reduce decision fatigue. If you walk past an activity station or a cooking space that's already set up, you're more likely to engage with it. The familiarity builds trust and removes that initial barrier of 'I don't know where to start'. I've seen residents who never used to join in start grabbing a Theraband or sitting in for meal prep just because the space invited them to.

The key is not to overwhelm the house with health messages or clinical-looking gear. It's about subtle cues. A fruit bowl in the middle of the table. Calming artwork on the wall. Speakers that play soft music in shared spaces. These things tell people, 'This is a place where we value health, calm, and connection.'

I'm not saying that environment solves everything. But when the space reflects the outcomes we're trying to achieve, people are more likely to move in that direction. We've seen it time and time again. When homes feel lived in, purposeful, and supportive, residents are more engaged. Staff are more motivated. And the home becomes more than just a service. It becomes a community.

Support Workers as Gateways to Wellness

Support workers are the single biggest influence on whether the home environment supports health or just ticks a box. You can have the best-designed house in the world, but if the culture in the house isn't right or if the staff don't feel supported, you won't get the outcomes you're aiming for.

In my experience, most support workers want to do the right thing. They want to help participants live better lives. But they're often stretched, overwhelmed, and lacking the tools to make that happen. When you don't have structure or resources, that pressure spills over. It affects the culture of the house. It affects the energy. And it absolutely affects the participants.

One of the biggest barriers I see is the assumption that staff should just 'know' how to deliver wellness. That they'll naturally guide participants toward better habits. But if you don't know how to play soccer, how can you teach it? If you've never been shown how to support someone with nutrition, how are you supposed to start?

That's why we built Able Digital Wellness. We had support workers telling us, 'I want to help, but I don't know where to begin.' So we created something simple. Activity prompts. Structured programs. Bite-sized resources they could actually use on shift. Not more training modules to complete after hours, but tools they could pick up and run with. The more support workers are empowered, the more they become the gateway to better outcomes.

It's not about giving them more to do. It's about giving them the right things to work with. A suggestion card for a 10-minute breathing exercise. A visual prompt to guide a quick prep session in the kitchen. A tracking sheet that helps link what they're doing to a participant's NDIS goals. These tools aren't just helpful, they're essential.

And when support workers feel confident, they become more engaged. When they start to see the results, fewer incidents, more participation, better moods in the house, they start to enjoy their work more. That reduces churn.

It reduces stress. And it creates a better environment for everyone involved.

I've also learned that if you want to change the culture in a home, you need to start with the staff experience, not just the participant experience. If your staff walk into a home that feels clinical, disconnected, or disorganised, that's going to shape their energy and how they interact with residents. On the other hand, if they walk into a space that feels calm, purposeful, and supported, they're far more likely to show up with the right mindset.

I always say that the house itself can create the conditions, but it's the people inside it who bring that to life. Support workers are the frontline. If we want to see real, lasting change in health outcomes, we have to invest in them. Not with more paperwork or more pressure, but with better systems, better tools, and better recognition of the impact they have every single day.

The Economic Case for Healthier Homes

There's a perception in this sector that wellness is a nice-to-have. Something extra. Something you focus on once all the essentials are sorted. But I've found the opposite to be true. When you prioritise wellbeing in the home, everything else gets easier: staff retention, incident reduction, participant engagement, and even compliance.

We've seen it firsthand. When a house feels calm and purposeful, staff are less likely to call in sick. Participants are less likely to have behavioural incidents. That means fewer incident reports, fewer investigations, and less emotional labour for everyone involved.

In one group of homes, we introduced very basic preventative health routines. Things like structured morning walks, nutrition-themed nights, and using one space in the home to encourage light movement. Within six months, there were fewer ambulance call-outs, fewer days off due to stress, and fewer Workcover claims. The data spoke for itself. But more importantly, the culture in those homes shifted. People were talking, connecting, and participating more.

There's a real cost to neglecting the health environment in SIL. Staff turnover is expensive. Workcover claims are expensive. Replacing burnt-out support workers over and over again drains not only your budget, but your team culture. And when participants are disengaged or inactive, their goals stagnate. That leads to frustration from families, increased complaints, and eventually the risk of losing trust in your service.

So when people ask, 'Can we afford to make our homes healthier?' I ask the opposite. 'Can you afford not to?'

I also think we underestimate how much stress poor design puts on support workers. If the kitchen layout makes it hard to prepare food together, you lose opportunities for engagement. If there's no quiet space in the house so people escalate more often. Those things compound over time. So when you invest in thoughtful, health-oriented environments, you're also reducing the emotional load on your team.

Even something as small as introducing a consistent routine, like starting the day with music or offering a five-minute group stretch, can dramatically shift how a house runs. It builds rhythm, helps participants regulate, and sets a positive tone for the day. That's not fluffy stuff. That's preventative infrastructure.

We often measure success by compliance or occupancy, but those numbers don't tell you how well a home actually functions. A house can be full and compliant, but still toxic for both staff and participants. When you bring in wellness thinking, you're investing in the long-term health of your service. That shows up in retention rates, staff satisfaction, family engagement, and yes, even the bottom line.

Wellness isn't a bonus. It's a strategy. A healthy home reduces risk, improves staff stability, and drives better outcomes. That makes it one of the smartest financial decisions a provider can make.

Reframing Choice and Control

'Choice and control' is one of the cornerstones of the NDIS. But too often, I've seen it used as a way to justify inaction. A participant doesn't want to go outside? That's their choice. They don't want to eat a proper meal? That's their right. And while yes, autonomy matters, we have to ask ourselves, 'Am I offering real choice or just avoiding responsibility?'

In one house I visited, staff told me that Dan didn't like being outside. He sat on the couch most of the day, scrolling through his tablet, and refused to go on walks. But when we spoke to his family, they said, 'Dan used to love going to the beach. He loved fishing.' That's when it clicked for me. He wasn't saying no to being outside. He was saying no to the *way* it was being offered.

So we reframed the activity. Instead of 'Let's go for a walk,' we said, 'Let's go to the beach and see if we can spot some fish.' And guess what? He said yes.

It's not about tricking people. It's about connecting the offer to what matters to them. If someone loves music, don't ask them to exercise. Ask them to help put on a playlist and have a dance. If they're into art, invite them to paint outside on the patio. The goal is the same, but the frame makes all the difference.

We can't assume that a single 'yes' or 'no' tells the full story. Choice requires context. It requires options. It requires support. And sometimes, it requires creative thinking from the people around them.

The other trap we fall into is assuming that promoting health automatically limits choice. That's not true. You can still offer people options that are meaningful and health-supportive. Do you want an apple or some yoghurt? Do you want to walk to the corner shop or around the block? That's still choice. It just removes the option of sitting still all day or drinking a bottle of soft drink before breakfast.

Support workers often feel stuck here. They don't want to be seen as pushy. But reframing is not forcing. It's guiding. It's offering alternatives that still meet a person's goals, interests, and needs. The only way to do that well is to know your participants. What they used to enjoy. What lights them up. What they're most proud of.

It comes back to relationships. When you know someone, you know how to offer options in a way that lands. That takes time and intention. But once you get there, the outcomes are so much better. People start choosing things that support their own growth, and it no longer feels like a tug-of-war between support and independence.

I always say that choice and control doesn't mean standing back and hoping something good happens. It means standing alongside someone and helping them see all the options clearly, including the ones that will lead to a better life.

Scott Chapman

Innovation in Practice

Innovation isn't always about doing something big or brand new. Sometimes it's about taking what we already know works and finding a smarter way to deliver it. In Supported Independent Living, one of the smartest things we can do is make wellness easy to access. In my experience, technology and collaboration are two of the best ways to do that.

When we built Able Digital Wellness, it wasn't about replacing people or creating another compliance system. It was about giving frontline teams simple tools to support health, even when they were under the pump. Things like an iPad loaded with activity prompts. Pre-recorded mindfulness exercises. A three-minute movement routine. These are things that staff can pick up and use without extra training or pressure.

It's not perfect, and it doesn't need to be. What matters is that the tools are there, they're consistent, and they're linked to participant outcomes. If a support worker can say, 'We tried this breathing exercise twice this week, and I've noticed fewer outbursts from James,' then you're building real momentum. That's how you connect day-to-day actions with bigger health goals.

The same goes for collaboration. I've never understood why some housing providers and support organisations treat each other like competitors. We're all trying to support the same people. When we work together, the outcomes are better.

Some of our best programs have come from sitting down with hub providers and asking, 'What are you already doing that works and how can we support that in the home?' We don't need to reinvent the wheel. If a participant loves art therapy at the hub, let's make sure they've got materials at home. If they've built a routine around movement, we can reinforce that in the mornings or evenings.

Innovation isn't about more. It's about alignment. When the house routines, staff mindset, and external supports all point in the same direction, progress happens faster. People feel supported. Staff feel less confused. And the whole system runs more smoothly.

We also need to look beyond our own four walls. Tech partnerships can make a huge difference, but only if they're implemented properly. We once worked with a wearable device that tracked participant sleep quality and restlessness. It wasn't about micromanaging people, it was about giving teams insight. When you know someone hasn't slept, you support them differently the next day. You adapt your plan. That can be the difference between a great shift and a critical incident.

Of course, not all tech is helpful. Some platforms are too complex, or they add another layer of admin for staff. That's why we need to pilot things in real homes, with real workers and participants. If it doesn't make their lives easier, it won't last.

The best innovations are the ones that disappear into the background. They're the things that support good routines, prompt better decisions, and help the team feel more confident. They don't make noise, they just work.

Innovation in this space doesn't mean reinventing care. It means creating smarter connections between people, environments, and tools. And when we get that right, the impact is massive.

Action Steps for Providers

If you're reading this and thinking, *We're not there yet*, that's completely normal. Most providers are still figuring this out. Creating healthier homes doesn't happen overnight. It starts with noticing what's already there and choosing one or two things that can be done differently.

Begin by speaking with families, not just during intake, but through meaningful, open conversations. Ask what their loved one used to enjoy before structured supports came into their life. What brought them joy? What were they good at? These stories hold the key to offering options that feel personal, not generic.

Then, walk through your homes with a fresh perspective. Ask yourself, 'Does this feel like a place someone would be proud to live in? Are there signs of life and identity, or does it look and feel like a workplace?' Pay attention to the small details: the scent of food cooking, the layout of shared spaces, the artwork on the walls. You don't need major renovations. You just need to look with purpose.

Next, ask your support workers what's getting in their way. What tools are missing? What would help them support health and wellbeing more confidently? Don't assume they're unwilling; more often, they just don't have the structure or prompts they need to act. When you ask the right questions, you'll often uncover simple fixes.

Wellness can be built into daily routines in subtle ways. Play music in the morning. Create a calm corner with soft lighting and textures. Introduce a five-minute group wind-down before dinner. These aren't programs, they are habits. Over time, they shape the atmosphere of the house.

Look outside your organisation too. Connect with hubs, therapists, or day programs already supporting your participants. Find out what's working well, and echo it in the home environment. Consistency builds momentum. It helps participants feel safer and more understood across settings.

Finally, track what changes. Not with formal reports or audits, but with everyday observations. Are people more engaged? Are there fewer incidents? Are staff sticking around longer? Share those wins. Let your team see the difference they're making. That feedback loop is part of what keeps people invested.

Here's a simple checklist to help you take the first few steps. Use it in team meetings. Post it in the staff room. Let it guide your next few months.

Scott's SIL Health Kickstart Plan

- Ask families what participants enjoyed before SIL
- Walk through each home with a fresh eye. Would I live here?
- Tweak one or two environmental details (light, sound, furniture, layout)
- Invite support workers to suggest practical tools they wish they had
- Add one small wellness habit to the daily routine
- Connect with hubs or external providers for service alignment
- Trial one new idea or resource that supports wellbeing
- Observe and track one clear outcome over four weeks
- Share positive changes with your team

Creating better homes doesn't rely on big budgets or grand strategies. It comes from intention. Each small decision, what goes on the wall, how routines are framed, which voices are heard, adds up to something powerful. This is how we move from managing people to supporting them so they thrive. Not by adding more work, but by reshaping the spaces and systems that surround them every day.

Final Wrap-Up, The Future We're Building Towards

Right now, many SIL homes meet basic requirements, but we're still a long way from creating spaces that actively support health and happiness. The good news is that we already know what works; we just need to put it together with more intention.

I want to see healthy SIL homes evolve into complete ecosystems. That means integrating technology, using data to guide decision-making, providing personalised content, upskilling staff, and designing homes that reinforce wellbeing through their layout and feel. These pieces aren't separate. When they're connected, they create environments where people live better, longer, and with more independence.

Homes like these don't just meet compliance. They help people feel good. They reduce preventable illness, support longer life expectancy, and make both the NDIS and Medicare systems more sustainable by focusing on prevention instead of reaction.

That future is within reach. And when we get there, I think we'll ask ourselves why we didn't build wellness into the foundation from the very beginning.

I also want to see more collaboration between providers. Some of the best results I've seen came from support and housing teams working side by side, sharing tools and routines, and aligning around what helps participants thrive. We're all trying to support the same people, working together just makes sense.

Well-being should be part of everyday life in these homes. Cooking a fresh meal, going for a walk, checking in with someone's mood or energy, those moments don't need to be complex. They just need to be consistent.

Support workers should feel confident leading those moments. They need tools that work on shift, not just during training. And they need to feel valued for more than just keeping things running. When a support worker knows they've helped someone feel better, more connected, or more in control, that's impact. That's the work.

The next phase of SIL shouldn't be about doing more. It should be about doing what works, with greater clarity and connection.

CHAPTER 2
GETTING COMPLEX CARE RIGHT

BY CAROLINE YATES

Caroline Yates is the director and co-founder of *Specialist Nursing Services*, a leading complex care provider in Western Australia. With over three decades of clinical and leadership experience, she has shaped high-acuity models of care across homes, schools, and SIL settings.

Caroline is a driving force behind the WA Complex Care Alliance, championing quality, safety, and sector collaboration. She brings a unique blend of clinical expertise and strategic vision to advancing person-centred complex care.

• • •

CONNECT WITH CAROLINE AT:
WEBSITE: snservices.com.au
LINKED IN: caroline-yates-436934281

What is Complex Care?

In Supported Independent Living (SIL), there is a cohort of participants whose daily lives involve significant clinical needs. We're talking about people who require PEG feeding, bowel care, suctioning, diabetes management, seizure response, or tracheostomy care, not occasionally, but as part of their everyday routine. For these participants, the care has to be delivered accurately, consistently, and in a way that still feels like home.

This group represents a small portion of the overall system, but the level of risk attached to their support is high. It's not because the tasks themselves are inherently complex; many aren't technically difficult. The risk comes from the consequences of getting it wrong. That's what sets this model apart from typical disability support.

While NDIS funding allows for high-intensity supports, there's often a gap between what's funded on paper and what happens in practice. A participant might have the right budget and live in a High Physical Support SDA, but that doesn't automatically mean the support team is clinically equipped to respond to a blocked tube or recognise early signs of deterioration. The house design might be excellent, but that alone doesn't make it clinically safe.

Too often, support workers are left to manage high-stakes clinical situations on their own without immediate access to clinical backup. If they're uncertain or an early warning sign is missed, escalation can be delayed, and in complex care, that time matters.

Getting it right means building a structure around the participant. That includes clinical governance, proper delegation, ongoing education, and clear escalation. It's not just about having a care plan on file. It has to be lived and supported every day.

Delegation works when there's strong oversight. For this reason we have clinical nurse consultants and educators as part of our team. They provide training, review care plans, support the staff, and stay involved. The responsibility doesn't disappear. It shifts to a model where the nurse is still there, just not always in the room.

Staff need more than a list of instructions. They need clarity and confidence. If they're supporting someone with epilepsy, they should know what that person's typical seizure looks like. If they're giving insulin, they should be able to spot signs of a drop in blood sugar early. That level of care only happens when education is hands-on, ongoing, and backed by proper systems.

Complex care doesn't mean it's clinical in appearance. We're not trying to recreate hospitals in people's homes. The environment should still feel like a home. The support needs to happen in a way that doesn't make the person feel like a patient. This work takes planning. It isn't reactive. It's built around the participant. Staff are briefed, the plan is active, and everyone knows what to do when something changes. That includes the family and any external providers. No one should feel like they're figuring it out as they go.

The people we support still want to live full lives. Complex care should support that. It should never limit it. But the only way that happens is if the right systems are in place and the right people are involved.

That's what complex care means to me. Not more equipment. Not more policies. Just better structure and stronger support for the people who need it most.

Redefining Complex Care in Disability Housing

Disability housing wasn't originally designed for this level of clinical support. Most SIL and SDA setups are built around supervision and assistance with daily living, not ongoing medical care. So when we place someone with complex health needs into a home like that, things can break down very quickly if the right systems aren't already in place.

Complex care in housing means high clinical risk delivered by non-clinical staff in an ordinary home. That combination is what makes it different. It's not just the care task that matters. It's how the care is delivered in an environment that isn't set up like a hospital. And it's done by support workers, not nurses.

That means we have to shift our thinking. We're not trying to remove the risk entirely; we're trying to make sure the right people are delivering the right care with the right support behind them. It's about planning for safety and delivering care in a way that still allows the person to live their life.

Support workers can absolutely do this work. I've seen them do it well. But only when the delegation is structured, the training is clear, and the clinical oversight is real. It can't be theoretical. If the person is being tube-fed or needs suctioning, the staff have to know exactly what they're doing. And they have to know who to contact if something isn't right.

Delegation isn't a one-off process. It's not enough to complete training and sign a form. We have to keep reviewing. Is the staff member still confident? Has the person's health changed? Are there new signs or symptoms we need to plan for? Delegation only works when it's active and supported.

That's why we use clinical nurse consultants and educators as a wraparound support. We build teams around the person so that staff don't feel alone. It's not just about compliance; it's about making sure care plans work in the real world, not just on paper.

The other part that is often missed is the environment. Just because a home is built to the High Physical Support SDA standard doesn't mean it's suitable for someone with complex health needs. That standard doesn't cover things like where to store clinical equipment, how to set up a room for a ventilator user, or how to create a space that feels calming and safe while still allowing for care to happen.

We've seen homes where the participant's bedroom looks like a hospital room. There's equipment everywhere, fluorescent lighting, machines out on display, and uniforms on the staff. That might feel safe to the family, especially if they've been running a mini-ICU at home for years, but often, it doesn't feel like home to the person living there.

We try to balance that. Yes, the care has to be visible enough that it's ready to go when needed. But we also need to bring the environment back to something that feels calm. Less clinical noise. Better lighting. Personal touches. Comfortable spaces. These changes matter. They help the person settle. They reduce anxiety. They make it easier for support workers to engage, not just deliver care.

It can take time for families to trust this process. And that's fair; they've often been the only ones caring for their loved ones. But when they see that the care works, that staff are trained and supported, and that the person is happier and more independent, they start to let go of clinical control. That's when we start to see real progress.

This isn't about minimising the risks. It's about managing them properly. That includes the physical environment, the clinical supports, and the confidence of the support team. When all of those are working together, complex care can be delivered well, and the person can live a much better life.

Creating Calm, Making Complex Care Feel Like Home

When someone with high clinical needs moves into supported accommodation, the first thing we look at is the environment. Not the equipment, not the plan, but how the space feels.

Creating calm is about taking a step back. What does this person need to feel at home? Where can we store the equipment so that it's close enough but not in their face? Can we change the lighting so it's softer? Can we reduce the noise from alarms or clinical conversations?

This doesn't mean hiding the care; it means being thoughtful about how it's delivered. The space should feel like it belongs to the person, not to the service. They should walk into their room and feel relaxed, not reminded of their health.

It also matters to the staff. If the environment is chaotic, it makes their job harder. If the room feels clinical, they default to clinical behaviour. That might include wearing scrubs, speaking in medical shorthand, or focusing more on tasks than on the person. All that creates distance and raises anxiety levels for everyone.

We work with teams to shift this. It's not about stripping everything back; it's about making decisions with the participant and their family. What needs to be removed? What can be stored differently? Can we create more privacy during care tasks? Can the person have more control over their routine?

These changes can feel small, but they matter. The way a home looks, sounds, and feels has a direct impact on a person's regulation and their sense of control. If we want to keep people safe, we have to start with helping them feel settled. That means thinking about how the day runs. If someone has multiple care tasks across the day, such as feeding, meds, and clinical monitoring, we try to build it into a rhythm that works for them. Not everything needs to happen at set times if it creates stress. We can often adjust routines to allow for more flexibility and more independence.

We also support staff to change how they think about documentation and communication. If everything is framed in clinical language, the person starts to feel like a case, rather than a person. That affects how they see themselves. We still document what we need to, but we focus on practical language that keeps the person at the centre. The goal is care that works, not care that looks impressive on a form.

Calm isn't just about the physical space; it's about trust. The participant needs to trust that they'll be supported without being smothered. Families need to trust that the care will be delivered properly, even if it looks different from what they've done at home. Staff need to trust that if something goes wrong, they'll be backed up.

Once that trust is there, everything runs more smoothly. Health outcomes often improve. People take more control. They become more social. They engage with their environment. And staff feel more confident, which reduces turnover and burnout.

If we get the environment right, we create a base for good care. Calm doesn't mean passive. It means stable, consistent, and respectful. That's what makes a house feel like home, even for someone with very high needs.

What Providers Get Wrong

A lot of providers step into complex care with the best intentions, but they don't always understand what's involved. It's not about effort, it's about knowing where the pressure points are and building the right systems to manage them.

The biggest mistake is thinking a policy or a nurse on the books is enough. Having a clinical escalation plan written down doesn't mean your staff know how to use it. Having a delegation form signed doesn't mean the team is ready. You need to check whether the care plan works in practice, not just on paper.

When something goes wrong, it usually comes down to one of three things: the person providing the care wasn't confident, the system didn't support them, or the escalation didn't happen in time. In complex care, that delay can have real consequences.

Training is often rushed or done once and never followed up. That's not training, that's a checkbox. We need to start with education that is hands-on, repeatable, and matched to the participant. You can't train someone on generic seizure management and expect them to feel ready for a person whose seizures present differently every time. The training has to reflect the real risks, not just the theory.

Then there's documentation. I've seen care plans with so much detail that no one reads them. Pages and pages of procedures look great in a policy manual, but make no sense at 3:00 am when a support worker is trying to respond to something they've never seen before. Documentation should be clear, short, and useful. If a support worker doesn't know what to do next after reading it, the plan has failed.

Delegation is another area where things often go wrong. People treat it like a handover. It's not. It's a shared responsibility. The nurse might not be there, but they're still accountable. That means they need to be reachable. They need to be checking in. They need to know the team and the participant. If the delegation is real, the nurse stays connected.

If staff are scared to escalate because they think they'll be blamed, they'll wait too long. If they don't feel supported by their clinical lead, they won't call. If the expectation is that they'll just 'figure it out' because there's no one else to ask, they'll shut down. That's how people get hurt.

Good care relies on good relationships. The staff need to feel backed. The families need to feel heard. The clinical leads need to stay involved. You can't fix this with paperwork. It's about how people work together day to day.

There's also a misunderstanding about what complex care costs. Some providers assume that because the participant has high-intensity funding, the margins are better. What they don't factor in is the cost of doing it properly. That includes regular training, clinical oversight, backfilling when experienced staff are off, and building time for care coordination. If you're not budgeting for that, the service won't hold.

I always ask providers the same set of questions when they say they're ready to take on complex care:
- Have you worked with this level of clinical risk before?
- Who is providing the delegation, and how often are they reviewing it?

- What does your on-call clinical support look like at 2:00 am?
- Can your staff explain the escalation pathway without looking it up?
- When was the last time the plan was tested in a real incident?

If you don't have clear answers to those questions, you're not ready. That doesn't mean you can't get there, but you need to slow down and build it properly.

The other thing I see is overconfidence. A provider will deliver support for one participant with diabetes or epilepsy and assume they're ready to scale. But not every case is the same. Just because you got through one situation doesn't mean your systems are strong. Sometimes things went well by luck, not structure.

The safest providers are the ones who stay curious. They keep asking questions. They take feedback. They look at what's not working and fix it before it becomes a risk. They don't hide mistakes. They use them to get better.

It's okay to say, 'We're not set up for that yet.' That honesty protects the participant, the staff, and the business. Complex care isn't something you grow into on the fly. It takes planning, investment, and leadership.

If you want to get it right, start with one person. Build the team properly. Set up the governance. Test the plan. Learn from it. Grow slowly and deliberately. There are no shortcuts. But when it works, it works well. The person is safe. The staff are confident. The family is supported. And the home feels like a place to live, not a risk to manage.

Caroline Yates

Building a Network Around the Work

You can only go so far doing this work on your own. You can build your clinical systems, train your team, and get the care right for one person, but if you're the only provider in your area doing it properly, that person still ends up stuck. Discharge is delayed. Funding doesn't match. Other services don't know how to work with you. You can't change that by fixing your own house alone.

That's why we set up the WA Complex Care Alliance. We needed a space where people doing this work could talk to others who understood what it involves. Not just the clinical parts, but the real experience of delivering high-risk care in a home, with support workers, under NDIS.

It's not a consultancy, it's not a top-down model. It's a group of people already doing the work who want to do it better. Providers, clinicians, educators, families, support workers. People who know how hard this is and want to share what they've learned.

In complex care, you're constantly solving problems. Things change fast. The plans don't stay still. Support needs shift. What works for one person might not work for the next. But instead of sharing that learning across the sector, most providers end up dealing with it in isolation. Everyone's doing the same work, just behind separate walls.

The Alliance gives us a space to bring that learning together. It's practical. What are we doing that works? What's broken, and how did we fix it? What can we share so someone else doesn't have to learn it the hard way?

It also allows people to say when they're not ready. That matters. There's a lot of pressure to look like you've got everything under control, but this type of work doesn't always go to plan. Support workers leave. Health needs change. Delegation fails. If you can't say something isn't working, you can't improve it.

In the Alliance, we test ideas and tools. Things like handover templates, delegation checklists, training frameworks. We try them in real environments, then bring the feedback back into the room. It's not theory. It's based on what happens when you're delivering care at 2:00 am, when the clinical lead isn't on site, and the participant starts to deteriorate.

We also involve clinical experts who understand disability. Nurses who delegate well. Diabetes educators who know how to make information stick. People who can support teams over time, not just come in for a training session and leave.

This kind of support should already exist across the system, but it doesn't. The NDIS has made disability support providers responsible for more and more clinical care, but the structures around that haven't kept up. Hospitals discharge people into SIL without a handover. GPs don't always know what providers are dealing with. And the responsibility lands on people who aren't being backed properly.

The Alliance gives us a way to close some of those gaps ourselves. Sometimes it's about getting a local health service to explain their expectations. Other times, it's helping a plan manager or support coordinator understand what complex care actually involves. It's also about helping new providers recognise when they're not ready, and what to put in place before they take that step.

We're not trying to scale a single model. We're building connections so people don't have to keep starting from scratch. If a provider in one region figures out how to manage enteral feeding safely with their team, why shouldn't someone else benefit from that? If a family has a good experience because communication between hospital and home worked, how do we make that normal, not the exception?

This work is complex. There's no fixed solution. But if we stay isolated, the people with the highest needs will keep getting the weakest service. That's not something we can solve alone. And we shouldn't have to.

The WA Complex Care Alliance is one way to shift that. Not by taking over. Not by blaming. By giving people a place to be honest, to learn, and to build together.

This is slow, practical, real work, but it's the work that keeps people safe.

The Future of Complex Care in SIL

We're going to see more people with complex needs coming into disability housing. That's already happening. People are living longer, leaving hospital sooner, and choosing to live in community-based settings. The needs are higher, but the support systems still look the same.

Most SIL models weren't built for this. They were designed around supervision, not clinical decision-making. So now we're trying to fit higher-risk care into a system that was never set up to hold it. Providers are being asked to carry that risk without the backup they need.

This isn't something that can be fixed by individual services on their own. We need the sector to shift. We need better support for the people delivering the care, and better connections with health services. Right now, providers are expected to deliver delegated clinical care, but access to nurse educators, clinical leads, or escalation support is inconsistent. It depends on your location, your budget, and who you know.

We also need to start training differently. Support workers are already doing a lot of this work, but often without enough preparation. If we want them to deliver care safely, we have to support them properly. That means clear training, regular refreshers, and access to someone who can answer questions in real time. It also means backing them when something goes wrong, and learning from it. We need to make education the foundation of everything we do, and what that brings to the staff and the participants.

There's room for more specialised roles too. We're seeing more services bring in clinical nurse consultants or educators who can stay involved over time, not just come in for one training block. These roles can help keep delegation live, keep the care plans relevant, and keep the team connected to someone with clinical expertise.

Technology is improving, and that's helpful. We can now track health indicators more easily, support remote clinical input, and communicate changes across teams faster. But technology on its own doesn't keep people safe. It supports the care, but it doesn't replace good judgement, strong relationships, and consistent practice.

The shift that matters most is in mindset. Complex care is not just about risk. It's about the person. If we build strong systems around them, they don't just stay safe; they live better. We've supported people who were told they were too high-risk for SIL, and now they're studying, travelling, and building relationships. They're doing those things because their care is stable enough to sit in the background instead of taking over.

We need to stop treating this kind of care as unusual. It's going to be part of everyday practice for more providers. The sooner we accept that, the sooner we can start building the systems to do it properly.

We're not there yet, but we know what's needed. And we've got enough people doing the work well now to start building from that.

That's the future I'm working toward.

CHAPTER 3
MEETING THE PARTICIPANT WHERE THEY'RE AT
BY LUKE WILSON

Luke Wilson is the founder and director of *Paylos*, an NDIS-registered provider delivering innovative, relationship-based supports across Victoria. Luke has lived experience as an at-risk young person; frontline work across child protection, disability, and international community development; and formal qualifications in therapeutic practice and human services. He has a Bachelor of Arts (Ministry), Diploma of Therapeutic Life Story Work, and a Certificate IV in Child, Youth and Family Intervention.

Luke brings a rare depth of insight to his work. His background spans disability, mental health, AOD, and complex trauma, giving Paylos the capacity to support participants with highly complex needs through a trauma-informed and adaptable model. This integrated approach positions Paylos as a service that bridges gaps across sectors, delivering disability supports that are trauma-informed, mental-health-aware, and grounded in genuine human connection.

• • •

CONNECT WITH LUKE AT:
WEBSITE: paylos.org.au
LINKED IN: @luke-wilson-55a546276

Meeting People Where They're At

'Society grows great when old men plant trees whose shade they know they shall never sit in.'

People talk about co-design a lot in this sector, but most of the time it doesn't look like I think it should. It's become tokenistic, a word we throw into funding applications or care plans without asking what it actually means.

For me, co-design isn't an optional process or a box to tick. It's a worldview, a belief system. It's how we show up. It's how we view people. It's how we build trust with someone who may have very little reason to trust anyone. When it's treated as a surface-level obligation, it causes more harm than good.

Co-design starts by meeting the person where they're at.

Not where we want them to be.

Not where we think they should be.

We stop. We listen. We follow their lead.

Even when the pace feels slow.

Even when it's uncomfortable.

That's the difference between seeing someone as a KPI and seeing them as a person on their own journey.

When I say "meet someone where they're at," I don't mean it as a slogan; I mean it literally. If a person is sleeping on a mattress in a room with no power, and no support has ever truly stuck, that's where we begin. We don't start with a plan, a service agreement, or language about outcomes, we begin by meeting them where they are and waiting until they're ready to let us in.

We once supported a participant who had experienced multiple failed SIL placements marked by police involvement, critical incidents, and frequent breakdowns. Over time, their story became buried under layers of documentation, and people stopped seeing the person behind the paperwork. When we became involved, we did things differently. We slowed everything down. There was no pressure, no pitch, just consistency. We spent time sitting with them, talking about what truly mattered to them, not to us, and allowing a relationship to form at its own pace.

Eventually, they asked, "Are you going to make me move again?" We didn't offer a rehearsed response or a polished promise. We simply said, "Only when you're ready."

That moment captured what co-design really means. It begins with safety, not just physical safety, though that's part of it, but emotional safety as well. It's the safety to say no without fear of consequence, to take time before engaging, and to move forward through small, manageable steps rather than being pushed into big, unfamiliar ones.

We talk a lot about giving people choice, but real choice only exists when someone feels like they have the power to say no. If saying yes is the only option, that's not choice, that's pressure dressed up as opportunity.

The first phase of co-design for us is showing up without an agenda. No forms. No timelines. Just presence. We might go weeks before we even introduce the idea of support. And when we do, it's offered, not assumed. That's what builds trust. Sometimes that trust builds quickly. More often, it doesn't. And we have to be okay with that. We have to sit with the discomfort of not being able to 'fix' things right away. We have to be willing to plant trees, even if we'll never sit in their shade. Because when we push for progress before the relationship is ready, we lose the person. They might nod along. They might go through the motions, but the engagement isn't real, and the outcomes won't hold. That's not co-design, that's tokenism. It serves us, not them.

This approach isn't always easy to explain to funders or stakeholders. It doesn't always *look* like work in the traditional sense. But it is work. It's foundational. Because once trust is there, everything becomes possible. The person starts to tell you what they want, what hasn't worked, what they're afraid of. They start to make progress because it's theirs. Their journey. Their goals. Their story. And that's the difference, it's theirs to own.

Real co-design means we build *with* the person. We don't give them the illusion of control, but power in the process. We're honest about the constraints. We talk openly about what's possible and what's not. We use language that makes sense to them.

We don't rush to fill the space when they're not ready. This doesn't mean throwing out structure. It means using structure differently. We don't lead with systems, we lead with presence. And then we build systems *around* what the person wants and needs. Because when we rush, we're usually designing for ourselves, not for the participant. That's what it really means to meet someone where they're at. It's slowing down, listening more than we talk. Letting go of the idea that we're the experts.

And starting with the belief that the person knows more about what they need than anyone else in the room.

Luke Wilson

Honouring Pace and Building Trust

One of the most important things we can do is let people move at their own pace. It's about recognising what real safety looks like for someone who's had a rough experience with support.

We worked with a participant who came to us with a long history of failed services and escalating behaviours. His care team had described him using all the usual language: high-risk, non-compliant, complex needs.

But when we met him, what stood out most wasn't risk; it was exhaustion. His parents were burnt out from managing him around the clock. He was reactive to anything that didn't go his way, and the idea of trusting new workers, let alone moving toward independent living, felt impossible. In fact, independent living *was* the long-term goal in his plan. But to those around him, it seemed completely out of reach.

At first, we could only visit with his parents present. They needed to be nearby in case things escalated. We didn't talk about outcomes or try to introduce the goal straight away. We focused on presence.

We met him at home. We built safety, slowly, through playful connection. For the first month, we didn't leave the house. We just built trust. Eventually, he agreed to go to a nearby park, just us and him. No expectations. No agenda. As his confidence grew, we began visiting social settings like the arcade or laser tag, environments that felt fun, not clinical. Each interaction helped him practise emotional regulation in a way that felt safe and empowering.

We mentioned, gently, that we had properties he could visit if he was ever curious. When he finally asked to see one, we arranged it so no other participants were there. After a few visits, we timed one so he could meet others briefly, as they were arriving while we were leaving. A soft introduction at his pace. Later, we let him know that some young people choose to stay overnight. But we were clear, it was only an option. There was no pressure.

Eventually, on one visit, we said, 'If you'd like to stay tonight, you can, but we're also happy to take you home whenever you want.' And because he had true choice, without expectation, he chose to stay. That decision was his. That progress was his. And he's been with us ever since.

People often assume this kind of support is passive, but it takes real discipline to hold space without rushing to fill it. You're still showing up. Still being consistent. Still offering options. But you're doing it in a way that doesn't overwhelm, pressure, or direct the person before they're ready.

We kept things simple. He always knew who was coming, when they'd leave, and what to expect. We didn't build structure based on what we thought he needed. We asked what would feel okay for him.

Over time, he opened up. He shared what hadn't worked in the past. What scared him. We didn't try to fix it. We didn't try to turn those conversations into progress reports. We just listened and responded in ways that honoured what he was telling us. That's what trust looks like. Not agreement. Not compliance. Just enough emotional safety for someone to become curious again.

People often talk about engagement, but confuse it with participation. Someone might show up because they've learned that saying yes keeps things calm. But real engagement is when someone knows they can say no and still be respected.

It took time, almost two years of slow steps before anything looked 'stable'. But when it came, it was solid because it was built through co-design, not control. He didn't feel managed. He didn't feel assessed. He had control over how things started, and that changed everything.

Today, he's thriving. He's learned how to cook, navigate social situations, resolve conflict without escalation, and experience the outdoors. He's built friendships. He's built skills. And most importantly, he's built trust in others and in himself.

The team knows him well now. There are still rough days, but he knows we're not going anywhere. He knows we're not going to push him into the next step just because we think it's time. That's the power of co-design, not as a framework, but as a relationship. We don't need to move fast. We need to move honestly. And at a pace the person can carry.

Empathy Over Expertise

When I interview for these roles, I use role-reversal scenarios, asking candidates to imagine receiving personal care without being asked for consent first. The strongest workers put themselves in the participant's shoes and instinctively value respect and collaboration. Qualifications matter, but they're not the differentiator. Skills can be taught. Empathy and compassion are non-negotiable.

We've worked with support workers who came to disability without formal credentials but with an exceptional ability to see from other people's perspectives. They're calm under pressure. They stay curious. They know when to step in and when to give space. You can't teach that from a workbook.

When someone doesn't feel safe, they don't need a perfect intervention; they need presence. Someone who can sit with the discomfort, not fill the space, not try to fix it, just be there, and hold it well.

We invest in building teams who can do that. It starts before day one. We run scenarios during recruitment, not to catch people out, but to see how they think. In a difficult moment, what do they notice? Do they get defensive? Do they reach only for compliance, or do they ask what might be going on for the person?

We also pay close attention to language. How you describe someone's behaviour reveals how you see them. If a worker can say, 'It seems like they were trying to protect themselves', we have a starting point.

That way of thinking doesn't end at recruitment. It continues through onboarding and everyday practice. We use role-play, not to embarrass anyone, but to practise staying calm and connected when things get messy. It's one thing to say you'll de-escalate, it's another to do it while being shouted at in a small room.

The goal is never perfection; it's capacity. Can a worker reflect after a shift and notice what worked and what didn't? Can they repair when something goes wrong?

We also make space to talk about what's hard. This work brings up a lot. Without time for reflection, people bottle things up or blame the participant. Neither helps. We aim for a culture where someone can say, 'That was tough' and not feel like they've failed.

Empathy is the anchor of co-design. Without it, you can follow every policy and still miss the person. With it, policies stop being boxes to tick and become tools that support real human work.

That's the team I want around the people we support, not just people who know what to do, but people who understand why it matters.

Systems Without Losing Soul

We need systems. You can't run good support without them. But they can't come at the cost of connection. That's where things often go wrong. We build systems to manage risk, and they end up getting in the way of the relationship. The focus shifts to ticking boxes instead of being with the person.

I've seen support plans written in a way that the participant can't understand. Staff can't follow them. They don't sound like the person at all. But because they're documented, the service thinks they're covered. That's not support. That's just paperwork.

A system has to make sense to the people using it. The participant. The staff. The family. Everyone involved. If the plan doesn't sound like the person, if the process is so rigid that it creates fear or confusion, then it's not helping. It's just noise.

We're always reviewing our systems, not because we're trying to stay compliant, but because people change. What worked last month might not be working now. If we're not checking in, we miss that.

We've built systems that are simple and repeatable, but still flexible. When we create a plan, we do it with the person. We sit together. We use their words. We talk about what works, what doesn't, what they want to try. It takes longer, but it works better.

The same goes for staff processes. When something happens, we don't just say, 'Follow the procedure.' We ask whether the procedure made sense in that context. If a staff member feels unsafe or unsure, they need to know what to do, but they also need to understand why they're doing it. Otherwise, they're just following rules out of fear.

We had a new staff member join one of our houses, and during training, they asked a lot of questions. Not in a way that challenged the system, but in a way that showed they were trying to make sense of it. That's what we want. People who think. People who ask why. Not just people who say, 'This is how I was taught,' and repeat it.

We also ask staff and participants to help review the systems. What's not working? What's unclear? Where are things getting stuck? It's not always comfortable. Sometimes we hear things we missed, but that's the point. Systems are only useful if they're alive. If they can respond to feedback.

I've worked in services where the processes were so tightly held that no one could adjust anything without permission. That creates fear. It shuts down initiative. It also leads to people hiding things because they don't want to get it wrong. A good system doesn't make people disappear. It helps them stay connected. It supports judgment. It creates a structure that can hold complexity without flattening it.

We're not building policies to protect ourselves; we're building systems to support people. That includes staff. That includes families. That includes the person at the centre of the support.

When the system is working well, the house runs smoothly. The team feels confident. The person feels seen. You can feel when that's happening. It's calm. There's room for feedback. There's room for change. When it's not working, we try something else. We don't defend the system just because it's written down. We ask what needs to shift so it works in this house, with this person, right now.

That's what it means to build a system with soul. It's not about being loose. It's about staying connected to the reason we're here. The person.

Balancing Risk, Autonomy, and Accountability

This work is full of risk. You can't avoid that. The answer isn't to remove risk, it's to name it, share it, and support people to make choices within it.

Before we plan anything, we agree on parameters. What's in our control? What's in theirs? What's non-negotiable? What can we figure out together? Naming this up front prevents confusion later.

People deserve agency, especially when risk is on the table. Agency doesn't mean saying yes to everything; it means being honest about real choices and the consequences that come with them. That honesty builds trust.

Case Study, 'You be Me, I'll be You'

In a previous role as a case manager in the child protection space, I supported a young person who was removed from the family amid high-risk behaviours: regular offending, illicit substance use, and violent, aggressive episodes. This young person had over 100 criminal charges, and I regularly visited them in custody to transport them back to placement after they were bailed. One time when I visited them in remand, they said, 'I'm only doing this because you're not letting me go home to Mum.'

The core conflict was clear, their goal was to return home and live with their siblings. Our concern was the safety of those siblings, given current behaviours and child protection opening a case on them. This is where co-design mattered.

I said, 'You pretend to be me and I'll pretend to be you. My goal is to go home to Mum. Your worry is my current behaviour and the impact on my younger siblings. How would you support me to reconnect with family?'

What followed was their support plan, rules and goals in their own words. I could hear what mattered most (they missed their family) while also communicating our non-negotiables (safety at home, no violence, no substance-fuelled episodes around siblings, and compliance with statutory requirements). The young person, while playing the role of the case manager, showed me their understanding of their recent choices and how that impacted their case plan goal of reunification.

Co-design here didn't mean only their design; it meant shared design. The young person, staff, stakeholders, and family each brought legitimate aims and constraints. We were transparent about our duties and limits; they were clear about what they could own and what support they needed.

The young person designed a set of 10 rules they chose to live by, and, after three months of consistent engagement with care members and reports of positive engagement programs, child protection began the planning for reunification. Over a 12-month process, the young person worked towards returning to the family home. That young person is no longer offending, is no longer dependent on illicit substances, has stepped away from violent peers, has a job, lives with Mum, and has regular movie nights with their siblings.

Outcomes like these aren't guaranteed, but they're far more likely when people have real power in a plan that also protects what must be protected.

A Future Led by Participants

When I think about the next five to ten years of this work, I don't think about new models or funding changes first. I think about what it would look like if co-design weren't the exception anymore. If it wasn't something we had to explain or justify. If it were just the starting point.

That's where I want things to go, a sector where participants lead. Where services are shaped around people, not the other way around. Where trust is something we build on purpose, not something we hope appears later.

It doesn't mean services stop being responsible. We still hold duty of care. We still manage risk. But we do it *with* people, not *to* them. That shift changes everything.

Support workers would be trained differently. They'd learn to listen before they act. They'd be asked what they've noticed, not just what they've done. Clinical teams would work alongside support teams, not above them. Language would change. Documentation would become simpler, clearer, more useful.

We'd also stop treating every participant the same. The more we try to create one standardised pathway, the more we miss the person in front of us. We'd slow down where we need to. We'd move faster where the relationship is strong. We'd flex, because we'd trust the people we're working with.

This isn't just about values, it's about outcomes. When people feel seen and heard, they settle. When they trust their team, they ask for help earlier. When they can choose, they invest in their own support. That's how we get lasting positive change. That's how we stop recycling trauma.

The services I admire most are the ones that don't just *say* they're person-centred, they *show* it. In how they respond. In how they listen. In what they build.

If we want to future-proof this sector, we have to stop designing systems to protect ourselves and start designing them to support people. 'We must plant trees and be prepared to never enjoy their shade.' That's the future I'm working toward, a sector shaped by the people in it, not around them. With them.

The Practice of Co-Design

If I had to break co-design down into something practical, it wouldn't be a checklist. It wouldn't be steps to follow in a straight line. It would be more like a rhythm, a way of working that adapts to the person in front of you.

But for people trying to do this well, especially in SIL, there are some key things I keep coming back to. Not as a formula, but as a starting point.

1. Start with Presence, not Paperwork

Before you build anything, just show up. Don't come in with a plan. Don't talk about outcomes. Just get to know the person. Be consistent. Be on time. Follow through. If they say no, respect it. If they change their mind, stay open. That's the first layer of trust.

2. Be Honest About the Parameters

This is where a lot of co-design falls apart. We say the person is leading, but we don't tell them what's negotiable and what's not. That creates false choice, which leads to disappointment and mistrust. Be clear from the beginning. What's within the team's control? What needs to be worked out with others? What are the limits? People can handle boundaries. They can't handle being misled.

3. Let the Person Set the Pace

You might want things to move faster. You might feel pressure from the system or the team. But if you rush the relationship, you're not co-designing, you're managing. Let the person set the pace. That might mean things take longer. It might feel slow. But it holds better.

4. Build Systems Around the Person, not Over Them

This is where structure matters. You still need plans, procedures, documentation. But they should make the work easier, not heavier. If your support plan doesn't sound like the person, rewrite it. If your systems aren't helping your team respond well, change them. Good structure gives people confidence. Bad structure creates fear.

5. Choose Empathy Over Expertise

You can train someone to follow a policy, but if they don't care, it won't matter. The people who thrive in this work are the ones who can stay calm, stay kind, and stay curious. Train for skill, but recruit for values.

6. Stay in the Room When it Gets Hard

Co-design isn't just the good parts; it includes the conflict, the silence, the discomfort. When someone says they don't want what we're offering, or they push back, or things don't go to plan, that's part of the process. We need to stay present in those moments too because these moments matter the most and lead to the best outcomes.

7. Review Regularly, and with the Person

Plans are never finished. People change. Relationships shift. Teams evolve. If you're not checking in with the person, you'll miss when the support stops fitting. Don't wait for a crisis. Build feedback into the normal rhythm of the service.

8. Let the Person be the expert in Their Own Life

This sounds obvious, but we forget it all the time. We bring our models, our experience, our assumptions. But the person has lived it. They know what's worked and they know what hasn't. Our job is to listen properly and build from that.

This isn't a perfect system. It's not something you can roll out and expect to work the same way in every home, but it's how we stay close to the people we're here for. It's how we move from saying we're person-centred to actually living it.

Co-design isn't a tool. It's a way of viewing the world and people. And if we get that part right, everything else starts to fall into place.

CHAPTER 4

WHAT GOOD SUPPORTS FEEL LIKE

BY RYAN SIMON

Ryan Simon has lived experience in SIL and residential care, shaped by a challenging upbringing. He was defined by his diagnoses instead of his identity until he found an adventure company that saw him as a person, not a disability. Treated with respect and given time to grow, Ryan found his voice. Now a speaker at expos and conferences, he shares his voice to inspire the sector in what he's passionate about, and that's change.

• • •

CONNECT WITH RYAN AT:
WEBSITE: paylos.org.au
LINKED IN: @ryan-simon-77886b386

Being Put Somewhere That Wasn't Right for Me

I ended up in disability housing when I was 14. It wasn't because of my disability; it was family and mental health issues. Things were unstable at home, and child protection decided it wasn't a safe environment for me or anyone else in the house.

I was sent to a disability home out in Keilor East. I didn't live there long, about four months, but it felt wrong straight away. The house was designed for people with physical disabilities. I've got a neurological condition and mental health challenges. The staff weren't trained in this area, and it showed. From the beginning, I didn't feel like I belonged.

They talked to me like I was a baby. Like a brand-new puppy. Baby voice. Over-the-top tone. Like I couldn't understand what they were saying. I remember thinking, *Do they think I can't talk?* I can do daily tasks. I can hold a normal conversation. I just wasn't given the chance. I answered the questions they had, although they answered the questions themselves. They didn't hear what I didn't say.

That's the first thing that got to me. I wasn't seen. I was treated like a disability, not as Ryan. They grouped me in with everyone else in the house, even though we were completely different. I wasn't asked about what I wanted to do or what I needed to live a good life. I was just given care and wasn't set up to succeed. I was set up to stay in the same place (physically and mentally) as I already was.

No one taught me how to live everyday life. I was only shown how to go out into the community when someone was right next to me. I didn't learn how to order a coffee. I didn't learn how to get on a bus on my own. When I didn't have someone beside me, I had no idea what to do. I became anxious. I stopped going out. I stayed in my room.

It made me feel stuck, like I wasn't supposed to grow or do anything more than just exist. When you're treated like that long enough, it becomes normal. You stop trying. You stop hoping. You just accept it.

I used to be really good at a lot of things, like sport and school. I was even ambitious about the future because I thought I could be an entrepreneur. But people didn't notice. They were too focused on what I couldn't do, and told me to dream of a real job because my desire to become an entrepreneur was 'unrealistic'.

When people don't understand you, they make you feel like a problem. I was spoken down to a lot. People didn't even realise they were doing it. They asked me about medication and hygiene

like I was five. No normal conversation, just ticking boxes. When I tried to start a conversation, half the time it was redirected to something else to tick their box. It was like I was a test subject.

Eventually, I gave up on care altogether. I didn't want support. I didn't want people around me. I distanced myself from everything and stopped engaging with the system. I ended up in a really stuck place for quite some time. I was in and out of psychiatric units, secure welfare and the ER. The people I spent most of my time with were paramedics and police.

SIL is a place where you're supposed to achieve your goals, and are set up to live an independent life, or the most dependent life you can live. It's not meant to make you stay in the same place you were in when you entered SIL.

I want providers to understand that it's not just about the roof or the rostering. It's how you speak to someone. How you see them. If all you see is a diagnosis, if you assume someone is not capable, they won't become capable, they won't achieve anything. Your assumption becomes reality.

The Moment I Felt Like I Mattered

When all I saw was a void for my future, I had a conversation with my child protection case manager. She told me about this adventure company. I said it sounds cool, so I started sessions with them.

The very first time I met one of the workers there, he sat down next to me and said, 'There's a cool car meet in the city. Do you want to go?' That might seem like a small thing, but for me, it meant everything. As a 16-year-old kid, I was so happy to hear those words.

That was the first time I felt like I was seen. He made me feel like I had value, and that changed how I thought about myself.

After being with the adventure company, I started to see a big difference in my life. I started engaging in the community, making friends, using public transport, cooking/cleaning, etc. Most importantly, I was taught how to be independent.

I had my ups and downs while I was with them; not everything went smoothly. I was still stuck at certain points and didn't know what to do. But I was given guidance, and my voice was heard in the process.

That's what good support is, equality, not being seen as my disability. It's not anything fancy or too much to ask for. All we want is not to be treated like a test or another statistic, but as a person, as you would be with a friend. We want to be seen as normal, but we can't do that if you're separating us with your baby talk, or you're treating us like some sort of science project.

That's what good support feels like. It's nothing big. It's not even something we should be asking for. We just want equality.

What Good SIL Looks Like

It all comes down to whether the carers see your identity before diagnosis, or if it's diagnosis before identity. Whether they talk to you like you're a person. Whether they show up because they want to be there, and not because it's just a job.

One of the biggest things for me is being asked. Not told. 'Hey Ryan, how do you want to do this?' or 'Does this plan work for you?' Having choice in the conversation makes a massive difference. It makes me feel like my opinion matters. A lot of people in SIL don't experience that. They are managed. They are moved around. They are treated like their goals don't matter. And that's how they stay stuck. I've seen people just give up, not because they don't care, but because they're never given a chance to make a change in their lives. How are we not being allowed to have a say in our own lives?

In a good SIL house, you feel like you have a future. You're supported to do things on your own. You're encouraged to keep trying. Support should help you leave care eventually, not keep you in it forever. It should teach you skills, help you build confidence, and prepare you for life. If it's doing the opposite, something's wrong.

Providers need to listen to the people they're supporting, not just in meetings, but in the everyday stuff. Ask us how we're feeling. Ask us what we want to work on. And when we tell you, don't just nod. Do something about it.

Just because we've got a diagnosis doesn't mean we want or need the same things. Some people want independence. Some want stability. Some want both. The only way to know is to ask, not assume.

What works for me is having that balance, a place that feels safe, but also pushes me to the best of my abilities. Not in a harsh way. Just in a 'we believe in you' way. They also need to know it's OK to make mistakes because they're lessons in disguise.

Good support is about building someone up, not holding them down.

My Future and Yours

I currently work across all areas of media, including videography, photography, and both pre- and post-production editing. This is the field I want to stay in. I love seeing my work come together. I'm passionate about the art of creating content, and I thrive on the creativity and dedication it takes to bring videos and photos to life.

I want to speak at events to share my perspective, not just on the system, but also my story and what I'm passionate about. I know what good support looks like because I've lived through bad support. I've been ignored. I've been left out of my own life. And I've also seen what it's like when someone listens, cares, and includes you. That's the kind of support worker (person) I want to be, someone who sees people for who they are, not what's written in their file. Someone who has time for them, and isn't there because it's just a job, but because they want this person to succeed and become the best version of themselves. I don't want their diagnosis to define them.

In the future, I want to work as a mentor to young people who are going through tough times. I want to sit next to someone and say, 'Yeah, I get it. I've been there too.' Sometimes the only person you can really hear is someone who's walked the same path.

Support workers who have lived experience bring something different. It's not just empathy, it's understanding. It's knowing what it feels like to be talked over, to be left out, to be told what your limits are by people who've never lived your life. When you've felt that, you don't forget it. And you make sure the people you work with never feel that way.

When I was at my lowest, I didn't think I had a future. I thought I'd just be in the system forever. One conversation changed that. Someone saw something in me. Someone believed I could do more. That belief gave me the courage to believe it too. I want to pass that on, to be the kind of support that doesn't just help someone get through the day, but helps them build a life.

That's what good support feels like. And that's what I want to be part of.

Being Real is the Support

What I've learned through working with Paylos is that support doesn't need to be complicated.

When I meet someone new, I don't start with, 'What are your goals?' or 'What support do you need?' I just talk to them. I ask what they're into. Sometimes it's cars. Sometimes it's music. I try to find something we have in common. Once that's there, the trust starts to build.

That's why being real matters. When someone just sits with you and doesn't force anything, that's when you feel most supported. It's not about tasks or routines. It's about connection.

Sometimes we'll just sit on a park bench and talk about shoes. That's the whole session. And that's okay because the point isn't to tick something off, it's to build a connection.

I don't want to be the kind of carer who walks in and talks about tasks. I want to be the one who listens. Who knows when to say something and when to stay quiet. Who can tell when someone just needs to be around another person who gets it.

I think the best thing any support worker can do is stop performing. Don't try to be the perfect professional. Be someone the person feels safe with. If they trust you, they'll talk. If they feel judged and they're treated differently, they'll shut down. That's the difference between being there and being present.

Good support feels calm. It feels equal. It feels like a real relationship where you're not being told who you are, you're being asked. That's what I try to give people now. Not advice. Not answers. A voice. Time. Respect. The things I wish I'd had more of when I was younger. I think if more providers focused on this, a lot would change. Support isn't always about doing more. Sometimes it's about doing less.

PART 2

THE PULSE OF THE PRACTICE

The operational backbone of SIL: strong teams, reliable systems, and quality processes.

'You do not rise to the level of your goals. You fall to the level of your systems.'
—James Clear, Atomic Habits

CHAPTER 5
BUILDING STRONG FRONTLINE LEADERSHIP
BY DAVE WELLS

Dave is the general manager at Coastwide Community Care, and everything he does comes back to one simple filter: 'Would this be good enough for my own family?' That's how he approaches leadership, making sure compliance keeps people safe, but never letting it drown out the real heart of what they do: care, dignity, and connection.

Dave is passionate about building a culture where staff feel supported and valued, and where the people they support feel free to live life their way. For him, care isn't just a service; it's community, and being part of that community is what drives him every day.

• • •

CONNECT WITH DAVE AT:
WEBSITE: coastwidecommunitycare.com.au
LINKED IN: @dave-wells-a4a765

Why Frontline Leadership Makes or Breaks an SIL Home

In Supported Independent Living, it's easy to talk about policies, systems, and compliance, but none of that matters if the frontline leadership isn't strong. The house leaders, team leaders, and coordinators are the glue that holds everything together. They're the link between the mission and values of the organisation and what actually happens in the house every day.

Frontline leaders are usually the people with the closest connection to participants. They see the subtle changes that others miss. They pick up on a shift in mood, a new medical issue, or a quiet sign that something isn't right. Often, these things are caught in the moment, not in a meeting. That's why they're so critical. They carry the values of the business into the home in a way that's lived, not just spoken.

When leadership is weak, the cracks show quickly. I've had to step back into a house when a team leader wasn't strong enough to manage the daily realities of participants and families. That's not where I should be. I don't want to be running the day-to-day of an SIL house anymore. I've done that. But if the frontline leader isn't up to it, the whole place slides backwards. A house without strong leadership doesn't feel like a home; it feels like a place where people are parked. Participants notice that. Families notice it too. And soon enough, your reputation is on the line.

Weak leadership means houses that look untidy and chaotic. Washing isn't done. Staff are sitting on their phones. Rooms smell. Prospective clients walk in and see a service that isn't proud of itself. Once that happens, you're already behind. You're not going to win trust, and you won't win new clients either.

When leadership is strong, the difference is obvious. Right now, I have an SIL house I haven't stepped into for two months. I don't need to. My team leader there runs it with absolute ownership. She calls the participants 'her clients' and means it. She sets high standards, and if staff don't meet them, she removes them quickly. She works hard, but more importantly, she leads in a way that makes everyone else lift as well. That's when you know you have the right person in place.

Frontline leadership is also about accountability. If decisions aren't being made or if they're constantly being overturned to keep people happy, the house falls into dysfunction. Participants stop trusting the structure. Staff start playing the system. But when a leader makes clear, consistent decisions and stands by them, the culture becomes steady. People know what to expect. That's the foundation of a good home.

You can't run an SIL house by remote control. You need leaders on the ground who understand the participants, the staff, and the families, and who can hold it all together in real time. When they're strong, the whole system works. When they're not, nothing else matters.

That's why I believe the success or failure of an SIL home doesn't start with policies or managers in head office. It starts with the person leading the house. Get that right, and you're ahead. Get it wrong, and you'll spend all your time fixing problems instead of building something strong.

Skills That Matter

A good team leader in SIL doesn't need to know everything in a textbook. They need people sense. That means reading the room, noticing the details, and understanding what both staff and clients are really going through. You can't learn that in a classroom. You learn it by paying attention and by caring enough to see what others miss.

One of the biggest responsibilities of a team leader is standing by their decisions. Too many make a call, then overturn it the moment someone complains. Once that happens, you've lost authority. Staff learn that all they need to do is push back, and the rules will change. From then on, the house runs on personal preference, not consistency. If you've researched your decision and it's sound, stick with it. Be fair but be firm. Without that, you don't have leadership; you just have someone managing rosters.

Empathy is the other skill that can't be ignored. Leaders need plenty of it. If you don't take time to imagine life from a participant's point of view, you'll never lead effectively. I tell my team to 'live a day in their shoes'. Try experiencing the confusion, frustration, or limitations they face daily, and you'll understand why patience and compassion are essential. Leadership without empathy is just authority, and that's not enough in SIL.

I also expect leaders to invest in self-education. When I came across a client with Korsakoff's syndrome, a severe form of alcoholic dementia, I didn't know what it was, so I read everything I could. I learned the patterns, the triggers, the strategies that work, then I wrote clear instructions for staff so they wouldn't get pulled into constant arguments. That's what leaders do. They don't wait for someone else to hand them answers. They go looking. They learn, and then they teach their teams.

Managing people is harder than managing tasks. Many team leaders are technically skilled but struggle with the people side. That's where mentoring makes the difference. I check in with my team leader every day, not to micromanage, but to make sure she's not overwhelmed. Once a week, I sit down with her for four hours. We use that time to unpack challenges, talk through decisions, and build her confidence. It's not about giving her all the answers; it's about giving her space to find her own.

I also encourage mistakes. Not reckless ones, but the kind you learn from. Too many leaders in this sector are terrified of making a wrong call because, in the past, they've been yelled at or punished. That shuts people down. They stop thinking for themselves. I want the opposite. I want leaders who are willing to try, reflect, and adjust. No one gets better if they're scared of failure. My approach is, make the mistake, we'll fix it together. That's how real learning happens.

The right mindset for a frontline leader is a mix of strength and humility. They should be strong enough to make decisions and stand by them. Humble enough to listen, learn, and admit when they need help. It's not about being the loudest voice in the room; it's about being consistent, fair, and genuinely invested in the people you're leading.

Leadership in SIL isn't glamorous. It's not about titles, it's about people. The leaders who succeed are the ones who never forget that.

Systems That Set Leaders Up to Succeed

Strong leaders don't just appear. They need the right support, the right structures, and clear expectations. Too often in this sector, people are promoted into team leader roles and left to figure it out for themselves. That approach sets them up to fail. My job is to make sure they don't flounder.

One of the most useful tools I use is something called the 1-3-1 method. It's simple. When a team leader comes to me with a problem, they have to bring one issue, three possible solutions, and one recommendation. I even gave them green notebooks for it. If I see them walk into my office with a green book, I know it's a 1-3-1 issue. If they walk in with a scrap of paper, I send them back to work it out properly. The process forces them to think through problems before handing them over. Nine times out of ten, they solve it themselves before they even get to me. That builds confidence and stops me from micromanaging.

Mentorship is another structure that matters. I give my team leader four hours every week in my office. We go through challenges, unpack decisions, and plan improvements. It's not about doing her job for her; it's about giving her a safe space to grow into it. Without that time, she would be left to sink or swim. With it, she learns faster and feels supported. That's the difference between surviving in the role and thriving in it.

Consistency is also critical. I've seen providers where every house runs differently. That creates confusion for staff, especially when they move between houses. It also hurts the participant experience. My view is that leaders should share what works and create a unified approach. Team leaders are not competitors; they are collaborators. Their job is to make life better for participants, not to outdo the house next door.

Cross-training staff is one of the best ways to build this consistency. If a worker only knows one house, you're stuck when people call in sick elsewhere. But if staff are trained across multiple houses, you have flexibility. It also builds understanding. People see different approaches and bring back new ideas. Cross-training takes effort, but the payoff is resilience across the organisation.

Another thing that sets leaders up for success is giving them full access to the information they need. Too many providers hold back budgets, behaviour support plans, or even rosters from their team leaders. Then, when something goes wrong, it's the team leader who is blamed. That is unfair and unworkable. If you expect someone to lead a house, you need to give them the tools. Information is a tool. Without it, they're working blind.

I also run supervisions and ask my senior staff to create 12-month plans. Every month, we sit down and check progress. These plans act like KPIs, but they're owned by the leader. They tell me where they want to improve, and I hold them accountable to that. It creates rhythm and accountability without becoming just another tick-box exercise.

At the end of the day, structures should not smother leaders; they should free them. The right systems give clarity, confidence, and room to grow. Without them, even the best people burn out. With them, frontline leaders can focus on what really matters, supporting their staff and creating homes where participants feel safe, respected, and valued.

Culture, Retention, and Growth

Culture is not something you write on a wall; it's what people live every day when they walk into a house or a shift. Culture is shaped by frontline leaders more than anyone else. They set the tone. If they are strong, consistent, and fair, the house feels safe and steady. If they are weak or distracted, the whole team feels unsettled.

Good leadership directly influences staff retention. People stay in jobs where they feel valued, supported, and part of something bigger than a paycheck. I've had staff tell me they've worked for years without ever receiving supervision. No wonder they feel disconnected. That's why I've put structures in place to meet with every worker to make sure they understand the mission and values of the business. If people don't know what we stand for, they can't carry it into their work. When they do know, they buy in.

I recently rewrote the values for my organisation after months of thinking and rewriting. I refused to put out something generic. Values only matter if they're clear and lived. When I gave them to staff, I made it clear, this is how we work, and if you don't agree, we need to talk. Culture can't be optional. If you don't align with the values, you don't belong on the team. That sounds tough, but it protects the people we support and the staff who genuinely care.

Values-based leadership also means holding people accountable for what they've promised. If you sit in an interview and say you'll work anywhere, but three weeks later refuse to drive, you're out. I treat every client like family, and I expect staff to do the same. My son is my benchmark. If I don't trust someone to work with him, they won't work with anyone else in my service. That's not negotiable.

Strong leadership also boosts morale. Staff want to see that their work matters. They want recognition, not just pay. I've started toolbox meetings outside normal hours to highlight good work and talk about where we are heading. It gives people clarity about our goals and helps them see how their role fits into the bigger picture. When people feel connected, they give more.

Retention is not about throwing money at people; it's about building trust. If a house feels well-led, staff will stay even when the work is tough. If it feels chaotic or unfair, they will leave no matter what you pay them. Leadership creates that stability. Loyalty is built through consistency in how decisions are made, fairness in how people are treated, and openness in communication.

Real Advice for SIL Providers

If there's one thing I want SIL providers to understand, it's that frontline leadership is not easy. But the solution is not to back away from it. You need to lean in, give leaders what they need, and expect accountability in return.

First, stop hiding information from your team leaders. Too many organisations hold back budgets, behaviour support plans, or details about participants. Then, when things go wrong, they blame the team leader. That's unfair and is also bad business. If you want someone to run a house, give them the tools. Give them the information. A good leader will use it well, and if you're providing the best service you can, clients will stay. You don't need to run your business in fear of losing them.

Second, get smart about structure. Think about how houses are set up and how leaders are placed. If you have three houses on one street, you might not need three separate team leaders. One strong leader can cover that cluster and build consistency. On the other hand, if you have participants with high and complex needs, they may need a dedicated leader and team. Structure should serve the clients, not just the roster.

Third, create collaboration instead of competition. Too many providers pit team leaders against each other. That does nothing for the people you support. Leaders should be sharing ideas, learning from one another, and working together to improve outcomes. When leaders see themselves as collaborators, not rivals, the whole service improves.

Fourth, encourage leaders to learn the business side of the work. They need to understand that money is not unlimited. Every decision has a cost, and those costs add up. I once showed my team what losing two hours a day of funded support meant over a year. It added up to more than 40,000 dollars. When you show leaders the numbers, they start to think differently. They stop assuming there will always be more funding and start making decisions as if their own money is on the line. That shift in mindset is essential.

Fifth, support leaders through mentoring and development. Don't just promote them and hope they figure it out. Give them regular check-ins, practical tools, and the chance to test their ideas. Let them make mistakes and learn. A confident leader grows into a stronger leader. An unsupported leader burns out or walks away.

Finally, remember that leadership in SIL is not about titles, it's about responsibility. The person leading a house sets the tone for everyone else. If they're strong, consistent, and values-driven, the house feels like a home. If they're weak or unsure, the house becomes unstable. You can't fake this. You either invest in leadership or you pay the price in turnover, complaints, and poor outcomes.

My advice is simple: be transparent, build smart structures, encourage collaboration, teach financial awareness, and back your leaders with real support. Do that, and you give them a chance to succeed. Fail to do it, and you set them up to fail. The choice is yours.

The Future of SIL Leadership

When I look ahead, I don't think the future of SIL will be shaped by big policies or head office decisions. It will be shaped by the strength of frontline leadership. If the people running houses are supported, trained, and trusted, the sector will be in a better place. If they're left without tools, the problems we already see will only get worse.

The first change I hope to see is more transparency. Too often, providers keep information away from team leaders because they fear it will leak. They hide budgets, behaviour support plans, or funding details, then expect leaders to deliver quality outcomes. That's backwards. In the future, I want to see leaders trusted with the information they need. If you expect someone to be accountable, give them the full picture. When leaders are treated as partners instead of liabilities, the quality of care goes up.

I also see collaboration becoming essential. Right now, too many team leaders and houses operate in silos. They compete instead of sharing. That doesn't help participants, and it doesn't build culture. In the future, team leaders should be working together across houses, sharing what works and creating consistency. Collaboration is not weakness; it's how you strengthen the whole service.

Another shift that needs to happen is around financial awareness. The NDIS is under pressure. Medicare is under pressure. Sustainability matters. Strong frontline leaders will need to understand the business side of SIL. That means knowing how rosters affect budgets, how small changes in hours add up over time, and how to make decisions that balance care with cost. When leaders think as if the money is their own, they protect the service and make sure participants don't lose out.

Technology will also play a bigger role, not to replace people, but to give leaders better insight. Imagine a team leader who can track patterns in sleep, behaviour, or engagement and use that data to adjust support before things escalate. That's not science fiction; it's already possible. The providers who adopt tools like this wisely will be the ones who deliver safer, healthier, and more sustainable services.

The future also depends on how we grow new leaders. Too many potential leaders never get a chance because they are seen only as shift workers. We need pathways that move good support staff into leadership, with mentoring, training, and encouragement to self-educate. The sector changes too quickly for us to rely only on senior managers. We need a steady pipeline of people who are willing to step up and take responsibility at the frontline.

Finally, I want SIL leadership to be respected as a profession in its own right. These are the people who hold houses together, who balance family relationships, who protect participants, and who guide staff. Their role is not 'extra', it's central. In the future, we should see frontline leaders recognised, supported, and valued for the impact they have. Without them, SIL homes don't work. With them, they thrive. That's the future worth building: transparent, collaborative, financially smart, tech-enabled, and full of leaders who see this work as a calling, not just a job.

Learning Leadership the Hard Way

I didn't learn leadership from a manual. I learned it because I had to. My body was breaking down from years of frontline work, and I knew I couldn't keep doing it. So I walked into my manager's office one day and said, 'I want to learn what you know.' That was the start. From there, I took every chance I could to learn, ask questions, and take on responsibility.

What I couldn't learn from a manager, I taught myself. I read, researched, and looked for answers. When I hit the ceiling in one job, I moved to another to keep growing. Sometimes that meant taking risks. Sometimes it meant leaving people behind, but it was the only way forward. Leadership in SIL isn't handed to you. You build it by putting yourself in positions where you have to grow.

The lesson I want others to take from that is simple; don't wait for someone to give you permission to lead. Put your hand up. Ask for support. Look for mentors. When that's not enough, go and find the knowledge yourself. Self-education is not optional in this sector; things change too fast. You need to keep learning if you want to stay effective.

The future of SIL depends on strong frontline leadership, not managers in head office, not policies alone, but people on the ground who can hold a house together and make it feel like a home. That's where culture is set, where participants feel safe, and where staff decide whether to stay or leave. If we keep building strong frontline leaders, the rest will follow.

CHAPTER 6

CLAIMING AND ITS IMPACT ON THE BOTTOM LINE

BY JOSH PIX

Joshua Pix is a dedicated leader with a passion for helping Supported Independent Living (SIL) providers thrive. As the director of *Resolv*, he's committed to easing the operational and financial challenges providers face, ensuring they can focus on delivering exceptional care. Joshua's expertise lies in uncovering lost funding, improving compliance, and streamlining rostering, payroll, and claiming processes.

Under his leadership, Resolv has helped over 130 SIL providers recover millions in lost funding, resulting in stronger financial outcomes and better support for participants.

• • •

CONNECT WITH JOSH AT:
WEBSITE: resolv.com.au
LINKED IN: @joshuapix

This chapter draws on insights from more than 200 Supported Independent Living providers across Australia. Every finding, pattern, and lesson shared here comes from the front line: real providers, real claims, real consequences. The goal isn't to give you a checklist; it's to change the way you think about claiming as a business discipline.

Claiming as a Strategic Priority

Claiming is the submission to the NDIS or a plan manager for the support you have delivered. It is the primary source of income for a SIL provider and the foundation of sustainability. On paper, it is simple: deliver the supports, submit the claim, and get reimbursed. In practice, there are many ways it can go wrong. When it fails, none of the hard work across the rest of the business matters. When it runs smoothly, it drives stability, growth, and better outcomes for the people you support.

The reason claiming is so important is the pressure created by the Disability Support Worker Cost Model. This model dictates what you can charge and how much of that revenue is consumed by wages, overheads, and operations. When the numbers settle, most providers are left with margins of barely two percent. That is not breathing room; it is a knife's edge. In this environment there is no space for "close enough." Mistakes in claiming can determine whether a provider survives or fails.

The biggest trap is confidence. Too many providers believe they are already claiming correctly. After reviewing more than two hundred SIL operators across Australia, I found that every single one had errors. Some were small. Some were worth millions. The comforting assumption that "I provide an hour, I claim an hour" rarely holds true in execution.

Another costly illusion is treating SIL funding as a neat, even number, dividing total funding by fifty-two weeks and assuming the problems are solved. Providers tell themselves it will balance out across the year, but it rarely does. Funding is tied to what actually happens in the house, not an average. When rosters are built on approximations instead of reality, providers either overservice or under-claim, exposing themselves to both financial leakage and compliance risk.

Almost every SIL provider is leaking significant money. Funding and revenue are constantly falling through the cracks, often unnoticed. Imagine a house that delivers ten thousand dollars in supports but only claims eight thousand because of a mismatch between roster and funding. That is two thousand dollars lost each week, more than one hundred thousand dollars a year. On average, we find leakage of around twenty thousand dollars per participant. This is real money that should be improving lives, not lost to inefficiency.

The impact is not only financial. Poor alignment between funding, rostering, and claims directly affects participants. Consider a house with two participants where one is being over-claimed and the other under-claimed. When the plan is reviewed, the underclaimed participant may have their funding cut through no fault of their own. Errors in claiming can reduce future support.

At its core, SIL claiming is not a single task. It is a living system where rostering, funding, and claiming are intertwined. Change one and the others must adjust. A participant's needs evolve, a ratio shifts, or a passive overnight becomes active for a period of time. Unless those updates flow through the roster and the claim, alignment is lost. In dynamic houses, maintaining accuracy requires deliberate systems and constant vigilance.

Claiming must therefore be treated as a strategic priority, not an administrative chore. It connects finance, rostering, and service delivery. Providers who master this alignment are resilient. They understand their numbers, forecast confidently, and adapt quickly when circumstances change. Those who do not are trapped in a cycle of leaks and fire-fighting.

The reality is simple. Claiming has always been make or break, and that will not change. Only the providers who treat claiming as a discipline, not an afterthought, will still be standing five years from now.

Common Gaps and Risks

Several recurring gaps and risks lead to breakdowns in claiming.

1. The Importance of Alignment

Many providers underestimate the complexity of claiming. They believe it is about matching hours to funding and pressing submit. In reality, SIL funding is a web of shared supports, individual ratios, community participation, and shifting participant needs. Every element must align precisely with both the roster and the claim. When one moves, all must move.

2. The Process Gap

Even when leaders understand the complexity, they often lack the processes to manage it. A ratio changes but the roster does not. A passive shift becomes active for a week but the claim stays the same. Small errors compound quickly. By the end of a quarter, those "minor issues" can cost tens or hundreds of thousands of dollars. Without a disciplined, repeatable process and clear reporting, these issues are inevitable.

3. The Systems Gap

Technology is often mistaken for a solution. "We have a rostering system that drives our claims, so we are fine." You are not. Software only executes the logic it is given. If the roster does not match the funding structure, the platform will automate your mistakes. If staff are not trained to check claims, errors will slip through faster. Technology supports good systems; it does not create them. In a resource-stretched sector, updates to systems are often delayed or ignored, amplifying the problem.

4. The Ignored Rejection

One of the most preventable and costly errors is ignoring claim rejections. Rejections are not just administrative noise; they are signals that something is wrong. Wrong line item, mismatched hours, exhausted funding – each rejection points to a process flaw that must be fixed, not merely resubmitted.

5. The Cultural Cost

When claiming fails, culture follows. Staff lose trust in the system, rosters shift unpredictably, claims are challenged, and managers scramble to plug financial gaps. Anxiety spreads to stakeholders, plan managers, and auditors. Claiming becomes another fire to fight instead of a process that supports people. Weak claiming corrodes confidence from the inside out.

All of these risks — gaps in knowledge, process, systems, and culture — are preventable. Prevention begins when claiming is treated as strategic. That means constant financial visibility, investigation of every rejection, and training every team member to see how their daily actions affect revenue. Poor claiming drains more than money; it drains trust, energy, and focus.

Building the Right Systems

When providers ask where to start, the answer is simple: build the right systems before you grow. Growth without structure multiplies problems instead of solving them. If your claims are already leaking money, expansion will only amplify the losses. Process comes first; growth follows.

At the heart of every strong SIL business lies one truth: funding, rostering, and claiming are inseparable. You cannot fix one without touching the others. Finance may believe it simply processes claims. Rostering may think it only fills shifts. Service delivery may focus solely on support. Yet each action influences the rest.

Integration is essential, and true integration is not about software. It is about shared methodology — a system that recognises how each function affects the whole. When rostering adds 1:1 shifts without checking the funding pool, finance processes unsubstantiated claims. When finance changes codes without communicating, rostering continues scheduling against the wrong ratios. The failure is not intent but silence.

The fix begins with accountability and transparency. Finance, rostering, and service delivery must communicate regularly, not just when problems appear. Discrepancies should be reviewed before auditors find them. The tighter the communication, the fewer the surprises.

For fast-growing providers, this discipline can feel like a brake. The instinct is to expand first and "sort the backend later." But later is always more expensive. Retrofitting systems after scaling is like rebuilding a plane in mid-air. Stabilise before you scale.

A major part of stability is clarity in rostering. SIL rosters are living systems of shared funding, shifting ratios, and evolving support needs. A roster that is perfect today may be out of alignment tomorrow. Rosters require continuous review and real-time updates. If a passive overnight becomes active, record it. If a ratio changes, update both roster and claim. Without disciplined rostering, alignment is impossible.

Technology has a role, but it is not a saviour. Buying new software will not fix broken logic. Platforms only work when the underlying method is sound. If your process is flawed, technology will automate the mistakes faster and hide them deeper. Start with methodology, then layer in tools.

Ultimately, building the right systems is not a finance project but a cultural commitment. Every staff member must understand how their actions affect claiming. Every leader must champion alignment. When integration becomes part of your organisational DNA, errors fall, leakage drops, and participants receive uninterrupted support. Strong systems are not red tape; they are your safety net.

Financial Sustainability and Future-Proofing

Most SIL providers are not losing money because of dramatic mistakes. They lose it slowly through constant leakage. Ratios change but claims do not. Shifts are coded incorrectly and rejected. Staff are replaced but rosters remain outdated. Each issue seems small in isolation but together they cost millions. These leaks are invisible unless you look for them. Sustainability depends on using data properly.

The first step is understanding performance at the house level. Many providers rely on high-level reports that hide the details. Funding, rostering, and claiming must be visible side by side for each house. That is where the truth lives. If one house is leaking two thousand dollars a week, you will not see it in an organisational total. At the house level, the problem is clear and fixable.

House-level data also drives forecasting. When you know how each house performs, you can project growth with accuracy. You can ask: if we open another house with a similar participant mix, what financial outcome should we expect? If we change ratios or staffing, what is the impact? Forecasting is not guesswork; it is modelling based on real data. Providers who do this grow strategically, not recklessly.

The Disability Support Worker Cost Model defines the financial reality of SIL. About seventy-four percent of revenue goes to staff, twelve percent to corporate costs, twelve percent to operations, leaving around two percent margin. That margin is razor-thin. Every rejected claim, rostering error, and missed hour eats into it. Sustainability means protecting that two percent with discipline.

This also explains why providers often struggle to resource their finance and rostering teams. Margins feel too tight to justify extra back-office staff. Yet under-resourcing these functions is a false economy. Errors cost more than the salaries you save. Finance, rostering, and claiming teams are not overhead; they are revenue protection.

Leakage occurs in two directions. Overservicing delivers more support than funding allows. Under-claiming fails to recover what was delivered. Both hurt the bottom line. Overservicing burns resources unnecessarily, while under-claiming leaves money uncollected. The only solution is constant monitoring and rapid correction.

Future-proofing is about building systems that handle change. The NDIS will not get simpler. Funding periods have already shortened from twelve months to three, tripling reconciliation workload. More change will come. Providers who struggle now will struggle more later. The future belongs to those who build resilience today.

Financial sustainability in SIL depends on three things: house-level visibility, rigorous alignment, and a culture that treats finance as everyone's business. When you know where every dollar goes, when your systems keep funding, rostering, and claims aligned, and when every team member protects revenue, you give your organisation a fighting chance.

The Future of Claiming

If providers think claiming is hard now, they need to brace for what is coming. The direction is unmistakable: more administration, shorter funding cycles, and tighter compliance. The shift to three-month funding periods is only the beginning.

This change will reveal who truly controls their systems. If processes are not watertight, rejection rates will rise. If rosters lag behind reality, alignment will collapse. If finance teams are already stretched, the workload will push them to burnout. The NDIS is not increasing the model to match complexity. The pressure will only intensify.

Expect greater scrutiny, not less. Audits will become deeper, data validation more granular. This is not a reason to panic but a reason to prepare. Providers relying on manual fixes will not survive in the long term. The era of patching problems is ending.

The only sustainable path is to treat claiming as a strategic function. That means proper resourcing, clear leadership, and accountability across the organisation. It also means recognising when internal systems have reached their limit. For many providers, the scale and complexity of modern claiming exceeds what can be managed in-house. Engaging external expertise is not weakness; it is a commitment to sustainability.

Agility will define the next generation of providers. SIL environments change constantly. Rostering must evolve just as fast. Successful providers will rely on agile systems that update in real time, communicate changes instantly, and connect directly to claiming workflows. Agility protects both revenue and participant outcomes.

The future of claiming is not about survival; it is about competitive advantage. A provider who can demonstrate that every dollar is aligned, every hour delivered, and every participant supported as planned will stand apart. Families will notice. Participants will notice. Stability and trust will become your reputation.

Complexity is inevitable. Providers who prepare now, invest in systems, use data wisely, and seek the right expertise will not just survive the tightening environment; they will thrive in it. The future belongs to the disciplined.

Why Claiming Is Everyone's Business

Many providers still see claiming as a finance task. That mindset is the greatest blind spot in SIL today. Claiming touches everything. Rostering choices determine what can be claimed. Service delivery determines whether supports match funding. Leadership determines how quickly misalignments are fixed. Finance might press the button, but everyone else decides whether that button triggers accuracy or error.

Claiming is everyone's business.

A support worker who records a shift correctly protects revenue.

A team leader who updates ratios promptly prevents leakage.

A finance officer who investigates a rejection rather than resubmitting blindly saves thousands.

Every action either strengthens or weakens the business.

When claiming becomes strategic, the results ripple outward. The organisation gains stability. Leaders trust the numbers. Families trust the provider. Participants receive the support they are entitled to – consistently and confidently. Claiming is not about chasing money; it is an essential part of delivering safe, high-quality care.

SIL will always operate on thin margins. That will not change. What can change is the discipline with which providers protect those margins. Claiming may look like numbers on a spreadsheet, but those numbers decide whether staff are paid, participants are supported, and organisations endure.

CHAPTER 7
BUILDING TEAMS THAT STAY
BY CHARLENE WOODBINE

Charlene is an experienced, legally qualified industrial relations practitioner who commenced her legal career specialising in employment law in 2004. Charlene later brought her legal skills and experience to various industries in the private and public sectors, specialising in aged care, disability services, health and education, providing a full suite of industrial and employee relations and generalist human resources. She is committed to making employment laws accessible to businesses and providing reliable and practical solutions whilst supporting them to build their in-house HR capabilities.

Charlene is also an experienced company director, company secretary and trusted governance advisor.

• • •

CONNECT WITH CHARLENE AT:
WEBSITE: carisconsulting.com.au
LINKED IN: @ charlene-woodbine-79675b215

Why Training Matters for Retention

From my experience working with SIL providers, there are very clear links between training and staff retention in the disability sector. When staff are given the opportunity to learn and grow in an environment that fosters collaboration and learning, they're more likely to stay, and their learning experience is authentic, which, in turn, means they're likely to remain employed in your business. When staff feel their learning opportunities are stagnant, punitive, or that they're unsupported, they're more likely to look for employment opportunities elsewhere.

Creating Career Pathways

When an employer provides opportunities for staff to obtain qualifications relevant to their role, they're likely to remain employed in that business because they value their employer's time and resource investment in them personally. As a result, staff feel they're building something that matters for their careers, not just for their current role. While many providers emphasise soft skills, employers should balance technical skills training and soft skills, recognising that both are equally important. Staff want to expand their skills so they can feel equipped to perform their role with their current employer, but also remain relevant and experienced for future opportunities.

It's critically important to reframe how the sector views training. Too often, it's thought of as a compliance activity or something we do just to meet the needs of our workplace. Perhaps it's time to reframe training as an investment to lift the capability of the NDIS sector as a whole. In doing so, we're building interest and engagement, which fosters a sense that staff are growing with us, not just working for us.

Reducing Burnout

Another critical link is the impact training has on burnout. Disability support workers often feel worn out. The work they do demands a lot of resilience. When they lack training and supervision, that pressure grows. Robust and ongoing training makes staff feel more capable. They feel supported. That reduces stress and, in turn, improves job satisfaction. It can be the difference between someone staying in the role or deciding they've had enough.

Recognition and Professional Identity

Recognition and professional identity are also tied to this. In our sector, recognition and professional identity are often missing. Many staff don't feel that their work is seen as professional, and that undermines retention. Training can play a big role here, particularly when employers prefer micro-credentials (like short courses) and portable learning over traditional qualifications and formal learning. Short, targeted courses delivered in bite-sized formats are proving to be very effective. They are relevant. They are usable. And staff value them because they directly support the pressures they face day-to-day.

I believe this is one of the most overlooked areas. Sometimes providers assume that qualifications have to be long and formal, but it's often the targeted short courses that make the biggest difference. They give staff confidence and capability on the ground, where the real pressures exist.

Better training also means better support for participants with complex needs. When staff are equipped with the right skills, they can handle challenging care situations more effectively and with less frustration. That reduces errors, increases confidence, and improves outcomes. It also has an upstream effect. Managers feel more confident in their teams because fewer issues are being escalated. And when an issue does escalate, it's more likely to be one that genuinely needs higher-level attention.

Workplace Culture

A strong culture celebrates learning, supports mistakes as part of growth, and makes people feel it's safe to develop. When you create that kind of workplace, staff are far less stressed, far more satisfied, and much more likely to stay.

The summary is simple; great training reduces stress, builds capacity, enhances job satisfaction, and creates a culture where people want to stay. That is how you retain staff in this sector.

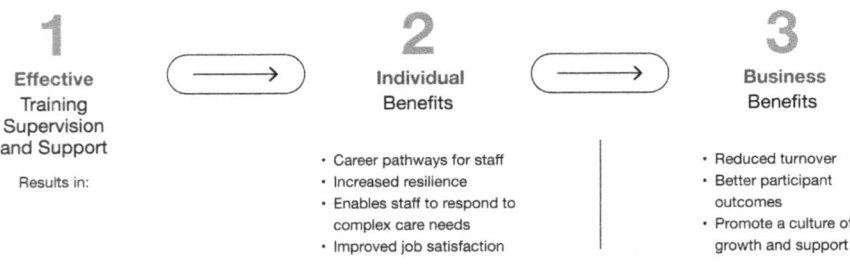

Charlene Woodbine

Designing Training That Works

As previously mentioned, one of the biggest challenges is reframing training away from just a compliance activity and treating it as a capacity and confidence-building exercise.

Too often, training is reduced to a box-ticking exercise. Staff may sit through modules, click through slides, and sign off on policies they may not have even read. That doesn't build skill. It doesn't engage staff, and it certainly doesn't help with retention.

Every day should be a day of learning and an opportunity to build training capacity. That doesn't mean staff need to sit in front of a presenter all the time; it means the workplace itself becomes a space where training is ongoing and connected to real situations.

For training to be effective, it has to be relevant to the role. That may sound simple, but it's often overlooked. Employers may be tempted to use easily accessible generic modules or off-the-shelf courses without considering whether the content reflects the work their staff are doing. The question should always be: what are the needs of our participants, and what skills do our staff need to support them? Once that's clear, training can be designed in a way that's intentional, relevant, practical, and meaningful.

One of the most effective approaches I have seen is the use of real-life scenarios. For example, one provider introduced a 15-minute case discussion at the end of every weekly team meeting. Staff could bring challenges they'd faced with participants, and the team talked through them together in a safe and open forum. In those short sessions, people shared strategies, supported each other, and learned in ways that were directly relevant to their work. Staff consistently reported that those 15 minutes were more valuable than a half-day workshop because it gave them something they could use immediately. Not only was the learning useful, but it built a sense of collegiality in the workplace where learning became a part of the day.

The notion of practical, on-the-job learning is not new but can sometimes be overshadowed by a preference for theory based learning. Providing practical, hands-on learning is critical. Role plays, skills practice, simulations, and on-the-job coaching are far more powerful than theory alone. When staff can practice in a supportive environment, they're more likely to feel confident when the situation arises in real life. That confidence reduces stress and helps them stay in their roles.

Coaching and mentoring should also sit alongside formal training to embed the content. Staff need someone they can go to when they have a question. It shouldn't be about managers handing out answers. It works best when staff are encouraged to bring potential solutions and then talk them through with a mentor. That builds initiative. It empowers people. It creates a sense of ownership in their work.

The other essential piece is embedding learning. Training can't be a one-off event that happens at induction or once annually. It needs to be reinforced, revisited, and lived in the workplace. That means creating an environment where it's safe to ask questions, safe to admit you don't know something, safe to learn from mistakes, all of which demonstrates a commitment to continuous improvement.

When providers design training with this mindset, they move away from compliance to real capability. Staff feel empowered, participants get better support, and the organisation builds a workforce that wants to stay and grow.

Defining Competencies	**Strategic Partnership**	**Learning Approaches**	**Foundational Integrity**	**Continuous Improvement**
What does excellence look like? Define core competencies	Partner with your stakeholders to renew, refine, & shape your training content	Implement blended learning approaches using in person learning and coaching on the job using real life scenarios	Incorporate compliance and quality standards	Review and Adapt your training

Section 3: Culture, Growth, and Engagement

Training doesn't just build skills, it builds organisational culture. When staff feel supported to learn, they see their workplace differently. They feel safe, valued, and recognised as professionals. That sense of recognition is often missing in our sector, and it's one of the reasons people leave.

When training is part of everyday practice, it creates a culture where learning is celebrated rather than mistakes being punished. Mistakes (within reason) are seen as opportunities for growth. Specifically:

- mistakes can reveal what the staff member doesn't yet know. This leads to deeper, more lasting learning than simply the pressure to get it right the first time.
- mistakes encourage staff to analyse their critical thinking skills by encouraging analysis and reflection on what went wrong.
- creates a safe working culture that signals a preference for progress over perfection.

This results in deeper learning and staff feeling that the provider wants them to succeed in a positive workplace culture and ultimately results in staff who want to remain employed in that workplace.

Staff feel they can ask questions without being judged. That trust is what keeps people engaged. If a worker feels safe enough to ask what might seem like a silly question, that is a sign of a positive culture. It shows they believe their organisation wants them to succeed.

This is where ongoing coaching and mentoring make such a difference. Formal training builds the foundation, coaching and mentoring cement it. They personalise the learning, give staff someone they can go to for guidance, and build relationships of trust.

I have seen how powerful this can be. One example comes from a large provider in Western Australia that was experiencing many challenges in the workplace, including high staff turnover, poor service delivery, team conflicts, and compliance issues. In addition, staff were managing a serious incident that left many staff traumatised, and the team leader resigned soon after. Staff were disengaged, stressed, and mistakes were being made.

The organisation responded by investing in trauma-informed practice training and providing counselling and supervision. They also supported an experienced support worker who stepped up as acting team leader, giving her a coach and mentor to build her leadership skills. The combination of training, reflection, and ongoing mentoring changed the workplace. Staff felt supported. The new team leader grew into her role, and the culture shifted from one of burnout and conflict to one of support and confidence.

Retention and Long-Term Impact

When we talk about retention, we often think about what it costs to lose staff. Recruitment costs are obvious and immediate, but there are deeper impacts too, on culture, on participant outcomes, and on the reputation of the provider. Training is one of the most effective ways to prevent that churn.

The link between training and long-term retention starts with career growth. People don't want to feel stuck; they want to see a path forward. When training connects to accredited qualifications, transferable skills, and specialist expertise, staff start to view their role as a profession rather than just a job. That professional identity is powerful.

Staff also want to know that their training has value beyond their current role. If a course gives them skills they can take anywhere in the sector, they're more likely to commit to their current workplace. It's the difference between training that feels like a hoop to jump through and training that feels like an investment in their future.

HR data provides important clues about how effective training really is. Exit interviews, turnover figures, absenteeism, and even patterns of sick leave tell a story. A sudden rise in absenteeism, for example, is often an early warning sign that something isn't working in the workplace. If staff are reluctant to come to work, it may be because they feel underprepared or unsupported. Training can address that by giving staff confidence and reducing the stress that makes them avoid shifts.

Tracking this data before and after training is critical. If turnover drops after the introduction of targeted training, that tells us the training is working. If staff report higher confidence in surveys, that's another signal. Providers should treat training not just as a cost, but as an investment to be measured.

Recruiting and onboarding a new staff member costs, on average, between $10,000 and $15,000. That includes advertising, shortlisting, interviewing, onboarding, and the time it takes for a new worker to become effective in their role. If a staff member leaves within their first year because they feel unsupported, that cost is essentially wasted and doubled as the recruitment process for a replacement commences. Retaining that person through good training would have been far more cost-effective.

High turnover also damages culture, brand, and reputation, as well as causing a loss of stability within teams. If teams lose stability, participants lose continuity of care. Managers spend their time plugging gaps instead of leading. This creates hidden costs that aren't always captured on a balance sheet. Training reduces these costs by building competence, confidence, and commitment in the workforce.

One of the biggest threats to retention in our sector is burnout. Current turnover sits somewhere between 17 and 25 percent annually in the disability sector, and burnout is one of the key drivers. That's an enormous figure. It tells us that almost one in four staff members leave each year, often because they simply can't sustain the pressure. The work is demanding. It requires resilience, emotional regulation, and the ability to manage complex care needs.

Training that builds resilience is not a nice-to-have; it's essential. Courses in resilience, communication, behaviour support, and supervision give staff practical tools to manage the pressures they face. Ongoing mentoring and reflective practice sessions provide the space for staff to process difficult experiences. This reduces stress, lowers burnout, and increases retention.

When training is missing or poorly delivered, the risks multiply. Staff who feel unsupported are more likely to leave, which drives up recruitment costs. Participants receive inconsistent care, which undermines trust. The provider's reputation suffers, making it harder to attract quality staff. Training isn't just about compliance; it's about breaking that cycle and creating stability.

If I could suggest one change that providers could make tomorrow, it would be to reframe how they see training. Too often, it's seen as something you do at induction or once a year for compliance. That mindset doesn't work. Staff rarely leave because they didn't get enough training in their first week; they leave because they feel unsupported as time goes on. Retention depends on what happens after the probation period, in the daily reinforcement, the ongoing mentoring, and the opportunities to keep learning.

Training should be evolutionary. It should grow with staff as they grow in their roles. It should adapt to the challenges they face and the goals they want to achieve. When training is framed in this way, it changes the whole experience of work.

Retention isn't just about wages or rosters. Those things matter, but they're not enough on their own. Retention comes from creating an environment where staff feel supported to learn, trusted to grow, and confident that they have a future in the sector. Training, when it is done well, is the foundation for that.

Practical Roadmap for SIL Providers

The question I am often asked is, 'What next?' Providers hear all this information about training and retention, then wonder how to put it into practice. I like to break it down into a simple three-month roadmap. It gives providers something tangible to follow, with the ability to modify and adapt without it becoming overwhelming.

Stage 1: Setting the Scaffolding (first four weeks)

The first month is about laying the groundwork. That means getting induction right and making sure it's not just about ticking boxes. New staff need training that's relevant to their role and linked to the needs of participants, as well as frequent check-ins. They also need to know where to go for support and who they can talk to when they are unsure. This is where establishing a mentoring relationship early on is important. In order to set the foundations right, it's critical that employers have a clear understanding of what excellence looks like in their business and the core components of the role. If there's no clarity on these points, it's impossible to set solid foundations in the first for weeks and, in turn, the training they receive and its links to the values and mission of the business will seem incongruent.

Stage 2: Embedding the Learning (weeks five to eight)

The second stage is where staff begin to put their learning into practice. This is where coaching, role plays, and reflective conversations really matter. It could be something as simple as 15 minutes at the end of a team meeting to share challenges and strategies. These moments give staff the chance to apply what they've learned in real situations, and to do so in a safe and supportive environment. It's about building confidence. Staff need to feel they can ask questions, try things, and keep improving without fear of being judged.

Stage 3: Feedback and Tracking (weeks nine to twelve)

The final stage is about checking in and measuring whether the training is making a difference. Staff should be asked what they found helpful, what still feels challenging, and what else they might need. At the same time, providers can look at HR data such as turnover, absenteeism, and incident reports. If those numbers improve after training, it's working. This stage closes the loop by making sure the training isn't only delivered but also evaluated and improved for the future.

To make this easier, I have developed a simple three-month training roadmap template that sets out each of these stages in clear, bite-sized steps. It can be adapted to fit different organisations, but the structure stays the same: start with foundations, embed the learning, and then check that it's working. Providers can download this tool and use it as a guide to begin building a stronger training culture in their workplace.

When you use a roadmap like this, you aren't just investing in compliance, you're investing in your people. You're giving them the tools to succeed, the confidence to grow, and the motivation to stay. That makes all the difference to staff, to participants, and to the future of your organisation.

The Bigger Picture

We have to be honest about the risks when training is treated as a tick-box exercise. Poorly trained staff feel overwhelmed. They make mistakes, they burn out, and they walk away. That leads to higher turnover, higher costs, and more instability. It creates stress for managers, inconsistency for participants, and reputational damage for providers. When participants and families lose trust, they take their business elsewhere. In a sector where word of mouth matters so much, that can be devastating.

When training is delivered well, the benefits flow across the whole organisation. Staff are more capable and confident. Managers feel supported by their teams instead of constantly firefighting. Participants receive better care because staff have the skills to manage complex needs safely and respectfully. Families feel reassured. And the provider builds a reputation as a good place to work and a trusted organisation to engage with.

Training is also about culture. A workplace that values learning sends a clear message: you matter, your growth matters, and we're in this together. That message is the difference between a staff member who stays and one who looks for the exit.

Culture isn't built through slogans or posters on a wall; it's built through what people experience day to day. The future of retention in the NDIS sector depends on this shift. We need to move from thinking about training as compliance to thinking about it as strategy. Compliance will always be there, it's a baseline, but strategy is what creates growth.

This isn't about creating complicated systems; it's about being intentional. It's about linking training to participant outcomes, staff career pathways, and organisational values. It's about listening to staff when they say what they need and adjusting accordingly. It's about creating everyday opportunities for learning, whether that is a quick reflection at the end of a shift or a structured mentoring conversation.

The business case is also clear. High turnover is expensive. Recruiting, onboarding, and losing staff again drains resources. Investing in training reduces those costs by improving retention. It also reduces risks around compliance, safety, and quality. When staff are confident and skilled, they make fewer errors, deliver better care, and create fewer problems that escalate to managers. That stability is worth far more than the cost of training.

Great training isn't an optional extra. It's the foundation of retention. It's what creates strong teams, reduces burnout, and delivers quality outcomes for participants. It's also what makes staff feel recognised as professionals, which is an area where this sector needs to improve.

We can't expect people to stay in roles where they feel unsupported and undervalued, but we can expect them to stay when they see a future, when they're given the skills to succeed, and when they're treated as people who deserve to grow. That is what training provides when it's done well.

Reframe training. Stop seeing it as something you do to stay compliant and start seeing it as the way you build culture, confidence, and retention. Make training part of your everyday practice. Create safe spaces for learning. Invest in your staff, not just for today, but for the future. When you do that, you'll build teams that stay, and when staff stay, participants benefit, families trust, and organisations thrive.

CHAPTER 8

SETTING A STRONG FOUNDATION WITH QUALITY PROCESSES

BY TANIA GOMEZ

Tania Gomez is a seasoned entrepreneur and certified auditor with a passion for empowering NDIS and education providers to navigate compliance with clarity and confidence. With nearly two decades of experience, she has founded and scaled four multi-million-dollar businesses, beginning her entrepreneurial journey at just 21. Her qualifications span education, disability, business, and regulatory compliance, giving her a rare, cross-sector lens that enables her to deliver strategic, tailored support to providers aiming for excellence.

Tania's consulting style is deeply practical and people-focused, rooted in her firsthand experience in both care and education settings. She combines sharp business acumen with a genuine drive to create meaningful, lasting impact in the NDIS space. Known for her holistic, innovation-led approach, Tania helps providers not just meet standards, but rise above them, building organisations that shine for their quality, culture, and contribution to community wellbeing.

• • •

CONNECT WITH TANIA AT:
WEBSITE: taniagomez.com.au
LINKED IN: @tania-gomez-5441bb80

Why Quality Matters in SIL

If you're running a Supported Independent Living (SIL) service, you're not just running a business. You're running someone's home. It's where people sleep, eat, relax, recover, and live their daily lives. That means the standard isn't just about service delivery; it's about dignity, safety, and trust. There's no room to wing it. You can tick all the compliance boxes and still have a home that doesn't feel like one. That's why quality matters.

The truth is, compliance is the bare minimum. I've seen providers pass audits while their team is stressed, homes are disorganised, and risk is one mistake away from becoming real harm. That's because compliance is about what's on paper. Quality is about what's happening in practice—how your systems support staff, protect participants, and hold the whole thing together. Without that foundation, things unravel quickly.

Quality isn't about being perfect. It's about building systems that make it easier to do things properly. When a provider has real quality behind the scenes, you see the difference. The team isn't scrambling when an audit is coming. Participants are calmer. Staff turnover drops. Decision-making gets faster and more consistent. And when opportunities come to grow or improve, those providers can take them without it all falling over.

I always say this to clients: the best investment you can make in your SIL business isn't a shiny new software platform. It's your systems. A good system doesn't just help you pass an audit. It helps your team know what to do on a Wednesday afternoon when someone's called in sick, the fridge is leaking, and medication needs to be signed out. That's when quality matters most.

In SIL, everything's interconnected. You're not just dealing with files and forms. You've got live rosters, food safety, tenancy obligations, behaviour support, medication, emergency procedures, and more, all happening inside real homes every day. If you don't have a strong system, the whole service starts to feel reactive. Staff get burnt out. Participants notice. Families complain. Auditors pick it up. It's not sustainable.

This is where people often mix up quality and compliance. They think they're the same thing, but they serve different purposes. Compliance is about meeting the rules so you can keep operating. Quality is about creating a structure that supports people to meet those rules every day without stress or shortcuts. Compliance gets you in the game. Quality keeps you there.

SIL brings a level of complexity that other NDIS services don't. Unlike community access or plan management, SIL providers are responsible for people's homes and daily living. That means you're also dealing with tenancy law, building codes, food safety regulations, fire safety, council inspections, workplace health and safety, and infection control. These responsibilities often exist outside what the NDIS Practice Standards directly cover, but they still apply.

I've worked with providers who thought they were doing fine until a fire inspector turned up or the council issued a warning for bin storage or maintenance. In some cases, they weren't even aware they were responsible for those areas. That's the problem with focusing only on NDIS compliance. It doesn't cover everything.

Good quality systems prevent problems before they surface. They help you spot issues early. Things like a fridge that hasn't been cleaned properly, a medication record that's out of date, or an emergency plan that staff don't know how to follow. These aren't usually one big crisis. They're a build-up of smaller things.

Most providers don't fall apart because of a single major event. It's the accumulation of small gaps, the missing shift notes, the forgotten maintenance jobs, the out-of-date support plans that gradually tip the service into risk. Without a system, you're relying on memory and goodwill, and that's not enough.

Quality doesn't mean everything runs perfectly. It means when something does go wrong, you know how to respond. You can trace the issue. You know who's responsible. You can fix it without panic. That's the difference.

People can feel when quality is working. They walk into the home and the environment feels calm. The kitchen is clean. Medication is stored properly. Staff know where the emergency plan is. Participants are comfortable. There's no chaos. That isn't an accident. It's a result of consistent habits, clear systems, and shared expectations.

You can't fake that. Referrers pick up on it. Families pick up on it. Participants absolutely pick up on it. If your service is only focused on compliance, you'll keep chasing problems. If you shift your focus to quality, you'll build something stable.

And here's the good news. It doesn't have to be complicated. It starts with doing a few key things consistently and doing them well. You don't have to overhaul your whole service overnight. But if you're ready to move beyond panic mode, and beyond band-aid fixes, then you're ready to build quality. That's where it all starts.

Tania Gomez

What Quality Looks Like in SIL Homes

Supported Independent Living isn't like other NDIS services. This isn't just about rosters and policies. It's someone's home. You've got people living together, sharing space, needing support around the clock, and expecting safety, dignity, and consistency. That means the bar for quality is higher.

You're managing more than support delivery. You're juggling tenancy obligations, behaviours of concern, medications, meals, emergencies, property safety, and legal requirements. And it all needs to come together in a way that works every single day.

The NDIS Practice Standards don't always give clear guidance for what this looks like in a real house. That's where a lot of providers get stuck. They have policies that say the right things, but those policies don't match what's happening in the home. That gap is where risk lives.

I've seen providers with beautiful documentation and yet, in the house, no one knows where the emergency plan is. Medications are being stored in the kitchen drawer. Risk assessments are all copied and pasted from a template. It looks fine on paper but wouldn't pass the sniff test from an auditor or a family member walking through the door.

So, what does quality actually look like in SIL?

It means your systems match your service. Staff are trained. Risk assessments reflect real needs. Documentation is current and accessible. Fire plans are on display. Medication is locked away properly. Shared spaces are clean and safe. And every person involved in the house knows what their role is and how to meet the standard.

That's not about being perfect. It's about consistency. The day-to-day rhythm of how your service operates is what determines whether you're delivering quality.

SIL is busy. Things change all the time. A staff member calls in sick. A new participant moves in. The fridge breaks. Plans change. Issues come up. If you wait for things to quiet down before addressing quality, you'll never get to it. That's why you need rhythm.

Good quality systems aren't about overhauling everything at once. They're built by doing small things regularly and building habits that last.

Start by breaking things down. Trying to fix every gap at once burns people out. Instead, look at what needs doing and build a simple structure around it. Make it part of your operations, not a side project.

Here's what I see work well for most providers:

- **Monthly:** Walk through each house with a checklist. Look at safety, cleanliness, medication storage, lighting, signage, and anything else that's out of place or potentially unsafe.
- **Quarterly:** Review participant files. Check support plans, risk assessments, incident reports. Make sure everything reflects current practice.
- **Every six months:** Review key policies. Are they realistic? Are staff actually following them? Do they reflect what's really happening?
- **Yearly:** Run a full internal audit. Bring someone in with fresh eyes if you can. You'll catch things you've stopped noticing.

The format doesn't matter as much as the follow-through. You can use a spreadsheet, a shared folder, or a checklist on your phone. What matters is that it's written down, tracked, and followed up. If it's not recorded, it didn't happen. If no one owns it, it won't get done.

You don't need new systems to do this. Most providers already have the tools. They just need to use them better. Add a quality check to your team meeting agenda. Review one file per week. Focus on one house per month. Give each team leader responsibility for checks in their home.

Small steps are better than big plans that don't get done. One house walkthrough is better than ten audits scheduled but never started. One clean participant file is better than five half-fixed ones. You just need to start.

The key is to build these tasks into your normal routines. That's how you create consistency. When your team sees that quality is part of everyday work, not a panic response before audit, they'll treat it that way too.

And make sure your staff understand what the standards actually mean in a house. Don't rely on policy documents to explain things. Do walkthroughs together. Talk through scenarios in team meetings. Ask real questions, like:

- Where's the fire plan?
- What happens if the fridge stops working?
- How do you store medication in this home?
- What happens if a participant refuses a meal or medication?

Make training practical. Role-play real situations. Make sure rosters reflect support needs, not just staff availability. If staff don't understand what compliance looks like in practice, they can't be expected to meet it.

The best quality systems are simple and consistent. They're not complicated. They're realistic. They make it easy for staff to do the right thing and hard to do the wrong thing. That's where you want to be.

Culture plays a role here too. If your team never hears about quality unless something goes wrong, they'll see it as a punishment. If they hear about it regularly, if they see progress, and if they're included in the process, they'll start to care. They'll bring things up. They'll suggest improvements. That's when you know the culture is shifting.

You don't need to micromanage. But you do need to be involved. Leaders should be walking houses regularly, reading inspection reports, reviewing documentation, and talking about quality in meetings. If no one at the top is asking about it, it will slide.

Build the rhythm. Keep it visible. Make it a habit. It doesn't need to be complicated. But it does need to be real.

Culture, Environment, and Audit Readiness

You can have all the policies in the world, but if your culture doesn't support quality, the standards won't hold. Culture starts with leadership. If the people at the top are disengaged or only show up when there's a crisis, it sets the tone for everything underneath.

Staff follow what they see. If leaders check in on homes, follow up on issues, and talk about quality often, staff will care more. If leadership ignores problems or cuts corners, it gives permission for everyone else to do the same.

You don't need a big program to change culture. It comes from consistent action. Do you walk the houses? Do you check files? Do you talk about what's working and what needs to improve? That's what matters. That's what people notice.

Bring the team in. This work doesn't sit with one person. Let team leaders take responsibility for checks in their homes. Give them ownership over their spaces. Ask for their feedback. When people feel like they're part of the solution, they take more care. Culture isn't about slogans or posters on the wall. It's about what gets followed through.

If something isn't working, name it. Don't avoid it. Call it out, decide on one thing to improve this week, and start there. Quality doesn't improve because people try harder; it improves because leadership shows up consistently and supports the right habits.

One of the biggest indicators of a strong quality culture is the condition of the home. In SIL, the house is the service. If the environment is chaotic, unclean, or unsafe, nothing else matters. That's the lens participants, families, and staff experience every day. And it's one of the first things an auditor will notice.

You don't need to wait for audit to get this right. Make house checks part of your regular rhythm. Once every quarter is a good start. Walk through the home with a checklist and a team member. Look at everything from entrances and lighting to fire safety equipment and bathrooms.

Are the exits clear? Are the smoke alarms tested and tagged? Is the medication stored correctly? Does the fridge work? Are chemicals labelled and stored away from participant spaces? Is the laundry safe and accessible? Does the home look and feel clean?

You're not just meeting NDIS Practice Standards. You're also responsible for tenancy law, WHS, fire safety, council regulations, and health standards. The checklist should cover all of it. The more you integrate these into one practical system, the easier it becomes to stay ahead.

The physical environment is also the most immediate sign of what your service values. If a house is well maintained, feels calm, and has clear signage and safe equipment, it sends a message. Participants feel it. Staff respond to it. Families notice it. If the fridge is mouldy, the smoke alarm is broken, and there's no emergency plan in sight, that tells its own story too.

Don't let things slide. Make checks part of your week. Assign someone to follow up on what's found. Track what's fixed and what still needs attention. This isn't about perfection; it's about creating a baseline of safety, comfort, and respect.

Audit readiness should flow naturally from this kind of rhythm. It shouldn't be something you scramble for when the Commission sends you a date. It should be a byproduct of running your service well.

Too often, I see providers hit panic mode. Suddenly, they're updating every file, rewriting policies, and asking staff to read documents they've never seen before. It's stressful and unnecessary. You should never be surprised by an audit. If your systems are working properly all year, audit becomes just another step in the cycle.

Take control of your timeline. Know your registration expiry date. Put it in the calendar. Start preparing six to twelve months out. That way, you're improving systems at a steady pace, not rushing to patch them at the last minute.

Understand the standards, but more importantly, know how they apply in your service. Don't just copy what others are doing. Think about how your team meets each expectation in practice. If your documents say medication is locked, show where and how. If your risk assessments are individualised, they shouldn't all look the same. If your emergency procedures are up to date, staff should be able to explain them confidently.

Audit evidence doesn't need to be complex. It just needs to be real. Current files, documented issues, clear follow-ups, and staff who know what they're doing go a long way.

Review your systems regularly. Choose one house and do a proper walk through. Pick one participant file and check that it reflects what's really happening. Don't just spot check the cleanest file. Look for gaps, fix what's out of date, and set a plan for reviewing others over time.

Talk to your staff. Ask what's working. Ask what's not. Bring quality into meetings. Choose one topic each month and open the floor. How do we manage medication? How do we respond to complaints? How do we check on safety?

When quality becomes a normal part of everyday conversation, it stops being a scary event and starts being a shared goal. And when staff feel heard and supported, they're more likely to speak up, notice issues, and help improve the service.

This kind of consistency doesn't require more work. It just requires the right work, done at the right time. You don't need a consultant every quarter or a new app to track everything. You need a team that understands what matters and leadership that pays attention.

Audit readiness isn't about being perfect. It's about being prepared. And that starts with building habits that hold, even when things get busy.

Final Takeaways

Quality isn't something you do for an audit. It's how you run your service every day. It shows up in the homes, in the handovers, in how problems are dealt with when no one is watching.

If you want to run a good SIL service, you need strong foundations. That doesn't mean fixing everything at once. It means starting small and sticking with it.

Start with one house. One file. One conversation with your team.

You don't need to overhaul the whole business overnight. Focus on the basics:

- Do your houses feel clean, safe, and calm?
- Do your records match what's really happening?
- Do your staff know what's expected and why it matters?

The goal isn't perfection. It's consistency. Build habits that keep your service solid even when things get busy. When a house is checked regularly, issues are caught early. When files are reviewed often, gaps are easier to fix. When staff are part of the process, quality becomes normal.

You don't need new software or a big budget. Use what you already have. Keep it simple. Keep it moving.

If you know something isn't working, don't wait. Write it down. Make a plan. Let your team know what's changing and why. Most providers already know where their pain points are. The difference is whether they take action or avoid it until audit time.

Quality takes time, but the benefits are clear. Staff feel supported. Participants feel safe. Audits go smoother. Growth becomes possible.

And you? You sleep better at night because you're not guessing. You know the system works because you've built it that way.

PART 3
REIMAGINING INDEPENDENT FUTURES

Strategic insights, innovative models, and bold ideas reshaping what SIL can become.

'If you wait until you're ready, you'll be waiting the rest of your life.'
—Lemony Snicket (Daniel Handler)

CHAPTER 9
USING TECHNOLOGY TO OPTIMISE WORKFLOWS
BY DR HEENA SINHA CHEUNG

Dr Heena Sinha Cheung is a multi-award-winning entrepreneur, author, and community leader who brings together lived experience, business acumen, and a vision for meaningful change. She is the founding director of My Second Home, a thriving NDIS-registered SIL provider, and co-founder of *Simple AI*, where she helps providers streamline compliance and operations through innovative technology solutions.

In 2025, she also launched My Safe Circle, an initiative to empower children and families with tools to prevent childhood sexual abuse, including her debut children's book *My Safe Circle: Learning to Protect Ourselves*. Heena is the recipient of the Women Changing the World Award (2025), an honoree in Australia's 40 Under 40, and a Silver Rising Star AusMumpreneur.

Beyond her business achievements, she is recognised for breaking records as an independent senate candidate in Victoria, where she continues to advocate for survivors, small businesses, and stronger communities. Passionate about building systems that put people first, Heena's journey reflects her belief in compassionate leadership and bold action.

• • •

CONNECT WITH DR HEENA AT:
WEBSITE: thesimpleai.com
LINKED IN: @dr-heena-sinha

Technology That Solves Real Problems

When people hear 'technology in SIL', they often think of something complex, expensive, and out of reach. But technology isn't about gadgets or buzzwords; it's about solving everyday problems that drain time, energy, and resources. It's about freeing staff so they can do what they came into this sector to do, support people.

Support workers join this industry because they care about others. They want to make a difference in someone's life. Too often, their time is swallowed up by forms, duplicating notes, and long handovers. One worker ends their shift and spends 15 minutes on notes. Multiply that across sites, and it adds up to hours lost every day.

Technology can cut that time significantly. A simple digital handover tool can reduce a 15-minute process to five. At My Second Home, we cut handover time from 15 minutes to just five, giving staff back precious hours with participants. Notes are structured, searchable, and instantly available to the next worker. The care stays human, but the paperwork becomes digital.

The same applies to support plans. In many services, these are written once and then sit in a folder until the next audit. Staff are expected to keep them up to date, but the process is clunky and slow. With digital systems, updates can be made in real time, shared instantly, and linked directly to the participant's daily activities. That means when a participant's needs change, the plan reflects it immediately. Compliance becomes part of the workflow, not an afterthought.

Audits are another area where technology solves real problems. Many providers describe sleepless nights leading up to an audit, digging through paper files and chasing missing signatures. A well-designed digital compliance system makes every record accessible in seconds. Staff can see at a glance if something is missing. Instead of weeks of frantic preparation, providers can be confident they are audit-ready every day. That shift reduces stress for leaders and builds trust with families and regulators.

Technology also helps with duplication. In too many organisations, the same information is written three or four times in different places. A support worker writes notes in a diary. A coordinator types them into a spreadsheet. A manager re-enters them into a compliance system. Each duplication increases the risk of error, and every extra step wastes time. Digital systems can remove that duplication. Information is entered once and flows to the right people automatically. That's not just efficient, it improves accuracy and reduces risk.

The impact is not only operational. When staff spend less time on admin, they are less stressed and more engaged. They feel trusted and supported. That flows through to the quality of support participants receive. A tired worker rushing to finish paperwork is not the same as a worker who has time to sit with a participant and engage fully.

Technology isn't replacing people; it's giving them the chance to do what they do best.

Building the Right Tech Stack

Every provider is different, and so is every tech solution. The right tool for one organisation may not work for another. That's why building the right tech stack isn't about chasing the most popular platform; it's about finding the systems that fit your context, your scale, and your challenges.

The first question I ask providers is: 'What are you trying to achieve?' Too many organisations buy tools without a clear goal, and then wonder why adoption fails. If the priority is compliance, the solution should focus on document management, audit trails, and reminders. If the priority is efficiency, the focus might be rostering or time-tracking. If the priority is growth, integration across finance, HR, and service delivery becomes essential. The wrong fit is usually not a bad product; it's a mismatch between the tool and the problem.

Flexibility is another key factor. SIL providers operate in environments that change constantly. Ratios shift, participants' needs evolve, funding rules adjust. A rigid system that can't adapt quickly becomes a burden. The right system should be able to scale with you, whether you grow from three houses to 30 or shift into different support models. Customisation matters too. A tool that lets you tweak forms, workflows, and reports to suit your way of working will always create more value than one that forces you into a fixed template.

Cost is often the biggest barrier providers raise. On the surface, new systems look expensive. But the question isn't 'How much will it cost?'; it's 'What are we losing by staying the same?' Think about the hours staff lose to manual duplication. Think about the money lost when a claim is rejected because documentation is missing. Think about the time managers spend firefighting instead of planning. Those hidden costs add up. In many cases, they outweigh the subscription fee for a digital solution.

When I talk to providers about tech adoption, one of the most common fears is getting locked into a system that doesn't deliver. The best way to avoid that is to run pilots. Test a tool in one house or with one team before rolling it out across the organisation. Get feedback from staff, measure the impact, and see if it really solves the problem. A good tech partner will support that process and adjust based on what you learn. If a provider pushes you to buy before testing, that's a red flag.

The stack itself doesn't need to be huge. A few core systems can cover most needs: a rostering and workforce platform, a compliance and documentation tool, and a finance or claims system. The priority is integration. The right stack isn't about how many tools you have, but how well they work together. Integration reduces staff stress as well as saving money.

I've seen providers become overwhelmed by choice. The market is full of options, and it's hard to know which one will deliver. My advice is to simplify. Start with your pain points. Build the stack around solving those problems. Don't be distracted by features you'll never use. Ask for case studies. Talk to other providers. Find out what has worked in environments similar to yours. You don't have to reinvent the wheel.

Finally, remember that technology isn't just about systems; it's also about partnerships. A good vendor should feel like an extension of your team. They should understand the NDIS environment, respond quickly when issues arise, and keep you updated on changes. Too often, providers sign up for a platform and then feel abandoned. The right tech partner will guide you through onboarding, training, and ongoing support. That relationship is just as important as the tool itself.

Building the right tech stack isn't about finding a perfect solution; it's about choosing tools that fit your needs, that grow with you, and that reduce the pressure on your staff. When you get it right, technology stops being a frustration and starts being an enabler. It supports compliance, improves efficiency, and gives you confidence that your business is ready for growth.

Getting Teams Onboard

Technology doesn't fail because of the tool; it fails because of the mindset.

Even the best technology will fail if your people aren't on board. I've seen tools with incredible potential abandoned because staff were afraid of them, leaders didn't set the tone, or the rollout was rushed.

The first barrier is fear. Many frontline workers worry that technology will make their jobs harder or replace them altogether. Some see digital tools as 'extra work' on top of what they already do. Others are simply anxious about using systems they aren't confident with. These fears are real and understandable. Support workers come into this sector because they care about people, not because they want to become tech experts. If they feel that technology pulls them further from care, they will resist.

The way to overcome fear is communication. Staff need to understand why a system is being introduced, what problem it's solving, and how it will make their lives easier. Too often, providers focus only on compliance or efficiency. They talk about audits, risk, and cost savings. Those things matter, but they don't inspire the people on the floor. The message that resonates is this, technology is here to give you time back. It's here to reduce paperwork, shorten handovers, and make compliance part of the workflow. When people see that the goal is to help them, not burden them, they begin to shift.

Leadership plays a critical role here. I always say that a business mirrors its owner. If leaders are fearful, staff will be fearful. If leaders see technology as a distraction, staff will too. On the other hand, when leaders show confidence, use the tools themselves, and reinforce the benefits, staff are far more likely to engage. Change starts at the top.

Another common barrier is habit. People naturally stick with what they know, even if it's inefficient. A paper diary or spreadsheet feels safe because it's familiar. Breaking those habits requires consistency. You can't launch a new tool and then allow staff to fall back on old systems whenever they want. There has to be a clear transition plan and accountability. That doesn't mean punishing people; it means providing support, setting expectations, and reinforcing them until the new way becomes normal.

Co-design is one of the most effective ways to build ownership. If staff feel that a system is being forced on them, they will push back. But if they're involved in shaping how it's used, they are far more likely to commit. That can be as simple as asking frontline workers what frustrates them about current processes and showing how the new system addresses those pain points. It can also mean customising templates, forms, or dashboards to reflect the way your teams work. When staff see their feedback reflected in the system, it becomes their solution, not just management's decision. In one rollout, frontline workers told us they felt 'listened to for the first time', and that ownership transformed adoption.

Training is another area where providers often stumble. One session during onboarding isn't enough. People forget, they're overwhelmed, and they need reinforcement. The most effective training is ongoing, practical, and delivered in different formats. That might mean short video guides staff can rewatch at any time, quizzes to reinforce key steps, or regular refresher sessions. Training should also be built into supervision so leaders can check how staff are using the system and provide support if needed.

I also encourage providers to celebrate small wins. When a team reduces handover time by 10 minutes a shift because of a digital tool, acknowledge it. When an audit passes with zero issues because compliance is automated, share that success. Recognition reinforces that the change is worth it.

Getting teams on board isn't about forcing compliance; it's about building trust. Staff need to know that technology is there to help them, not to replace them. They need leaders who set the example, systems that are customised to their work, and training that supports them beyond rollout. Change sticks when people feel ownership of the solution.

Future-Ready Operations

Every provider wants to believe their systems are working well enough. But 'good enough' isn't a safe place in SIL. Margins are thin, compliance demands keep increasing, and participant needs are constantly changing. Systems that feel adequate today can be the thing that holds you back tomorrow. Being future-ready means spotting the warning signs early and making changes before the cracks widen.

One of the biggest red flags is shrinking margins without a clear reason. If your costs are rising but you can't pinpoint why, it often means your systems aren't giving you the visibility you need. You may be overservicing in one house and under-claiming in another. You may be carrying duplication that wastes staff time. Without accurate, timely data, you're making decisions in the dark, and that's not sustainable.

Another warning sign is when managers are drowning in paperwork. When leaders spend more time chasing documentation than leading people, something is wrong. I've worked with providers where team leaders spent half their week compiling compliance reports manually. Not only is that a poor use of their time, but it also creates risk. Manual processes are slow and prone to error. If your managers are buried in paperwork, they're not driving culture, supporting staff, or focusing on participant outcomes.

If the word 'audit' still sparks panic, your systems aren't future-ready. Providers who build compliance into daily workflows treat audits as routine check-ins, not survival tests.

One of the best ways to prepare for the future is to treat your business like a participant's health. We run regular health checks for the people we support. Providers should do the same for their operations. That means reviewing your systems, looking for duplication, testing data accuracy, and checking whether staff find the tools easy to use. Sometimes you can do that internally. Often, it helps to bring in external advisors who can see blind spots that are difficult to spot from the inside.

Advisory boards are another valuable tool. A well-chosen board brings in expertise that providers can't always access in-house. Finance, technology, compliance, governance, these perspectives strengthen decision-making. Even a small group, two or three trusted advisors, can make a big difference. It doesn't take a large board to build resilience.

Being future-ready isn't only about avoiding risk; it's also about creating space for growth. If your systems are clunky and inefficient, they'll stop you from scaling. Each new participant or house will feel like a burden instead of an opportunity. On the other hand, when systems are streamlined, growth becomes smoother. You can add houses without doubling admin. You can expand services without burning out managers. Systems should enable growth, not hold it back.

There are also smaller, practical steps providers can take right now. Review your meetings. Are they productive, or are they full of repetition and confusion? Technology can streamline agendas, track actions, and ensure follow-up. Look at onboarding. Is it rushed, inconsistent, or dependent on one trainer? Digital onboarding platforms can create consistency and give new staff confidence from day one. Review your handovers. Are they taking too long? Are details getting lost? Structured digital handovers save time and improve accuracy. These quick wins not only improve efficiency, but also signal to staff that the organisation is serious about continuous improvement.

The providers who thrive in the years ahead will be the ones who treat systems as a living part of their business, not a set-and-forget exercise. They will monitor, review, and adapt constantly. They will bring in advisors when needed and act on early warning signs instead of ignoring them. Most importantly, they will see technology as a tool to strengthen people and processes, not just as a box to tick.

Future-ready operations don't happen by accident. They are built with intention, maintained through vigilance, and strengthened by a culture that values accuracy, efficiency, and trust. Providers who commit to that work now will not only survive the pressures of the sector, but they'll be positioned to grow, innovate, and deliver even better outcomes for participants.

Dr Heena Sinha Cheung

Safety, Security, and Trust

For many providers, the biggest hesitation with technology isn't cost or training, it's safety. Leaders worry about data breaches, privacy risks, and compliance failures. These concerns are valid. We work with some of the most sensitive personal information in the country. If systems aren't safe, participants and providers both carry the consequences. Building trust in technology starts with addressing these fears openly.

The first step is to understand what secure technology looks like. At its core, it means that data is encrypted, stored locally or in trusted jurisdictions, and backed up in ways that protect against loss. It also means that access is controlled. Not every staff member needs to see every record. Role-based permissions ensure that people only view what is relevant to their work. Good systems make this easy to manage and audit.

Providers should also be curious and demand transparency from their vendors. Where is the data stored? How often are security patches applied? What certifications does the platform hold? Has it been tested against Australian privacy law and NDIS standards? Too many providers assume these boxes are ticked, only to discover gaps when an incident occurs. Be curious and demand transparency. If a provider hesitates, take it as a warning sign, and remember, you don't need to be a technical expert to ask. The right vendors will make safety and compliance clear, simple, and accessible.

Artificial Intelligence tools create another layer of concern. The rise of AI has raised questions about how data is collected, processed, and used. Providers need to be clear that any AI they adopt is compliant with privacy obligations, uses secure storage, and doesn't feed participant data into external systems. AI can be powerful for streamlining tasks like reporting or note-taking, but only if it's built responsibly. Before adopting AI, providers should ask: 'Is this tool built for our sector or is it a generic product being retrofitted?' That distinction matters for both safety and usability.

Building trust isn't just about systems; it's also about communication. Staff need to feel confident that the tools they're using are safe. Families need to know their loved one's information is protected. Transparency builds that trust. Providers who explain how data is secured, who share their processes, and who invite questions create reassurance. Hiding behind technical jargon only fuels fear.

Another practical step is regular training. Staff should know how to handle sensitive data, how to avoid phishing attempts, and how to report issues. Technology is only as safe as the people using it. Even the most secure platform can be undermined by poor habits if staff aren't aware of risks. Embedding data safety into onboarding, refreshers, and supervision is essential.

Trust also grows when providers demonstrate reliability. A system that crashes during audits or loses information quickly erodes confidence. Testing, backups, and vendor support all matter. Providers should know how quickly they can recover data if something goes wrong. They should also have clear escalation paths with their vendors. Confidence comes from knowing that if a problem arises, it will be addressed quickly and effectively.

Technology in SIL is about people. Safety and trust aren't optional; they're the foundation. Participants deserve to know their privacy is protected. Staff deserve systems they can rely on. Leaders deserve confidence that their compliance is secure. Choosing the right tools, asking the right questions, and building a culture of safety ensures that technology becomes an enabler, not a risk.

Be Brave, Start Small

When I think about technology in SIL, I don't see software or dashboards first; I see the people behind them. I see the provider who tells me about sleepless nights before an audit, worried they will miss something. I see the manager who spends hours every week copying the same notes into three different systems. I see the support worker who wants to focus on participants but feels buried in paperwork. These are the real challenges that technology is here to solve.

You don't have to do everything at once. Pick one problem that creates the most stress in your organisation and solve that first. If handovers are eating into staff time, start there. If compliance is your biggest fear, choose a tool that gives you audit-readiness. If duplication is exhausting your team, find a system that integrates. One step at a time creates momentum.

There's also no need to reinvent the wheel. Many of the problems you're facing have already been solved in other organisations. The systems exist. The processes exist. The knowledge exists. Reach out, ask questions, and learn from those who have been there before. Providers who isolate themselves often waste money and energy trying to build from scratch. Collaboration and advice can make the journey faster and less stressful.

What I hope providers take away is that technology isn't about replacing people, it's about giving them more space to do what they do best. When systems are working well, staff spend more time with participants. Leaders focus on strategy instead of paperwork. Families feel reassured that their loved ones are supported by an organisation that's stable and sustainable. Technology is the bridge that makes that possible.

The sector isn't getting simpler. Margins will stay tight. Compliance will increase. Participant needs will evolve. Providers who thrive in the next five years won't be the ones who resist these changes; they'll be the ones who embrace them thoughtfully, with systems that support their people and protect their future.

Be brave. Start small. Every step you take toward stronger systems is a step toward safer, more sustainable, and more human care.

CHAPTER 10
THINK BEFORE YOU ACT
BY CHRIS LAPA

Chris Lapa is an experienced growth strategist and passionate leader with over 12 years of expertise in scaling direct-to-consumer brands and early-stage startups. His career has been defined by a hands-on approach to driving sustainable growth across diverse industries, and he has successfully led teams and collaborated with external partners to optimise performance through data-driven marketing strategies. With a proven track record in managing omni-channel marketing initiatives, Chris brings a wealth of knowledge in areas such as business analysis, marketing strategy, and digital advertising.

Throughout his career, Chris has worked with top-tier companies including Nine Entertainment Co., Southern Cross Austereo, and Crowne Plaza Hotels, as well as partnered with iconic brands like Lexus, BMW, Phoenix Tapware, Caddy Australia, and Cricket Australia. His versatility in scaling businesses, from large corporations to sole traders, has made him a trusted expert in growth management. With a deep understanding of what it takes to accelerate a brand's success, Chris continues to inspire others by blending strategic insight with practical experience.

• • •

CONNECT WITH CHRIS AT:
WEBSITE: thegrowthacademy.com.au
LINKED IN: @christopher-lapa-36108055
INSTAGRAM: @chrislapagrowth

Start with Strategy

I've seen too many SIL providers fall into the same trap, launching into marketing without any real strategy. When there's a vacancy, or worse, multiple, they panic. I get it. Every empty bed is revenue lost. But reacting from a place of desperation leads to poor decisions. The default becomes turning on a Facebook campaign, chucking some money at Google Ads, or hiring a BDM, hoping one of those things will magically fill the vacancy. It rarely does.

The problem? There's no mapped-out journey, no customer segmentation, no unique messaging, and often, no understanding of the emotional drivers behind a decision as big as choosing a home.

The biggest mistake I see is focusing too much on you (the provider) and not enough on them (the participants, families, or support coordinators). I call it the 'we, we, we' problem:

We have a great house.
We have 24/7 care.
We support independence.

That's not marketing, that's a real estate listing. And it completely misses the mark.

Marketing is Emotional, not Just Functional

SIL isn't just about bricks and mortar. It's about home, and that means emotions. For families and participants, the process is often filled with anxiety, guilt, hope, and fear. If your messaging doesn't speak to those emotions, it won't land. If your images are generic stock photos or poor-quality snaps of empty rooms, you're doing yourself a disservice. This is someone's dream of a new life with expert care and community support. Show that. Show the warmth. Show the people.

Don't Forget the User and the Chooser

If there's one thing providers forget most often, it's this. Your audience isn't just one person, and it's never you. In SIL, you're not just talking to one audience. You've got 'users' (participants), but often, it's the 'choosers' (support coordinators, family members, guardians) who are driving decisions. Each of these groups has different fears, wants, frustrations, and motivators. Yet most providers blast out a one-size-fits-all message and wonder why it doesn't stick.

If you want to fill vacancies effectively, you need to tailor messaging and your approach. The support coordinator needs different information from the participant's mum. They need to receive it in different ways, on different platforms.

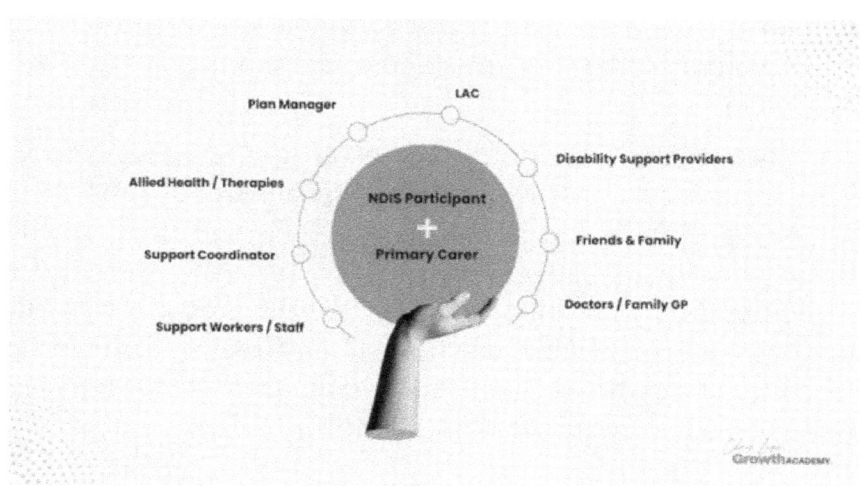

What's the Cost of not Stopping to Think?

Launching a campaign without a strategy is like trying to empty a leaking boat with a bucket full of holes. You might feel busy, but you're not making progress.

Before you spend a cent, you must ask:

- Who are we talking to? Who are we not talking to?
- What do they need to hear?
- Where are they on their journey? What do they need to get to the next step?
- What are the alternatives to us? (because there are plenty)
- Do we have the systems in place to nurture the enquiries and move them to choose to live with us?

If you don't know who you're connecting with or what you're trying to say, if your website isn't set up to convert, or your intake team isn't ready to follow up within 6 to 12 hours, you're possibly letting good opportunities fall through the cracks.

More often than not, **the better question** to ask is: 'Why wouldn't someone choose us?' That level of reflection, honesty, and unbiased perspective reveals the gaps. Maybe it's the poor-quality images, the generic copy, the alternatives in the area, or your support model simply isn't the right fit for that participant (and maybe you're attracting the wrong people to start with because you're talking to everyone). Plug those holes before turning on the tap.

Category	Our Company	Competitor A	Competitor B
Service Focus / Niche	Complex needs, psy-chosocial	Generalist supports	Youth supports
Specialised Training	Advanced behaviour support, trauma-informed care	Core training only	Allied health part-nership focus
Participant Profile	Ages 18–45, complex support needs	All ages, low complexity	Children and young adults
Response Time (Enquiry to Start)	Within 48 hours	7–10 days	5 days
Availability	Three locations, lim-ited immediate start	Immediate start metro-wide	Regional coverage only
Relationship with Families	Active, collaborative case meetings quar-terly	Minimal communication unless necessary	Monthly updates via email
Participant Progress Tracking	Quarterly goal re-views with partici-pants	Annual service report only	Ad-hoc feedback calls
Staff Consistency	Dedicated core teams assigned	Staff rotate weekly	Limited core team focus

Begin with Empathy

The first thing I get any provider to do is step into the shoes of their audience. Think about the emotional journey they're on. What fears are they trying to escape ('away-from' motivators)? What hopes are pulling them forward ('toward' motivators)? Your entire strategy needs to be anchored in that emotional truth.

When you truly understand your audience, you don't just 'promote a house'. You offer hope, growth, trust, peace of mind and somewhere to call home. And that's what people really want to buy.

Section 2: Audience & Journey Mapping

Take a moment to imagine being a parent trying to find a suitable SIL home for their adult child. It's not a casual process; it's emotionally loaded. They're worried. They feel guilt. They hope their child finds connection and safety. If your messaging doesn't see them, if it doesn't reflect their world and emotions, and doesn't prove you've done it before, it won't work.

Actions	Emotions	Decisions
Receives Autism diagnosis at paediatrician visit	Shock, worry, confusion	Starts googling or asking AI "what to do after autism diagnosis"
Reads articles, joins a parent Facebook group, spirals down AI rabbit hole	Overwhelmed, isolated	Realises there may be help but doesn't know where to start
Learns about the NDIS but feels intimidated	Fear of making mistakes	Decides to look for someone to guide them
A friend recommends a support coordination company	Hope, slight relief	Decides to call them nervously
Intake worker listens and explains calmly	Anxiety, cautious optimism	Chooses to book an intake appointment
Receives clear explanation of NDIS access steps	Empowered, supported	Commits to starting the access process
Books first NDIS planning meeting	Hopeful	Begins to feel more in control

One Journey, Many Decision-Makers

The journey to choosing an SIL home is rarely linear and never solo. As I previously mentioned, there are 'users' and 'choosers'. Participants, families, carers, support coordinators, allied health professionals, and even social workers in hospital discharge roles can all be involved. They each have different pains, needs, and questions, which means you need tailored messaging and smart segmentation.

You can't say the same thing to everyone and expect it to land.

And it's not just about the message. It's about where you're showing up. LinkedIn is great for support coordinators. Facebook and Instagram are where families scroll after dinner. Google Ads are where people go when they're ready to act. And yes, networking events still work, but you have to stand out. If you put the wrong message in the wrong place, it doesn't matter how good it is, it won't connect.

Journey Mapping in Practice

Customer journey mapping is something I work on deeply with providers. In SIL, it's essential. It's a complete view of every step, emotion, and decision point someone goes through and what support, information, and guidance they need on the way to choosing a SIL provider.

Here's how it typically looks:

1. Diagnosis/Future Planning

They start with a diagnosis or conversation about needing to find a home. They begin researching, online and offline. They're talking to LACs, Support Coordinators, GPs, and allied health professionals, and they ask:

- 'What is SIL?'
- 'What's the difference between SIL and SDA?'
- 'Are SIL houses safe for my child?'
- 'Who is the best SIL provider in my area?'

2. Awareness/Discovery

After they become comfortable with the idea and are ready to take the next step, they discover your brand or your competitors. This might be through:

- Social media ads
- Parent groups
- A Google or AI search
- Word of mouth
- Expos, networking events or brochures

3. Consideration & Comparison

This is where they dive deeper into understanding the landscape, reading and researching providers, and building a mental image of what a great SIL and a bad SIL look like. They check out websites, scroll your social media, download brochures, read reviews, and look at testimonials. They might be asking friends, family, or Facebook groups for recommendations.

4. Shortlist & Enquiry
At this point, it's about:

- Your team's warmth and professionalism
- The look and feel of the house and the support inside the home
- Values alignment
- Participant compatibility
- Availability and location

A good tour, quality photos, detailed and real client stories, or a strong brand video can make or break this phase.

5. Decision

Now it's about:

- Response time
- Follow-up processes
- Clarity of the onboarding steps
- Confidence in your support model
- A tailored approach to creating confidence with all users and choosers

6. Post-Move Support
This includes onboarding, welcome packs, family communication, feedback collection, and making sure the person feels like they belong.

7. Advocacy
Delivering exceptional care and support so that the user and their choosers become stark-raving fans. After all, the sector has been built on strong advocacy and referrals. Just because

you're looking at other growth options doesn't discount the importance of this! I hope that all providers continue to be so awesome that they don't need comprehensive marketing funnels, just a simple method to ensure that their name stays at the top of the list.

Channels	Step	People	Growth & Conversion Factors
Hospital	Crisis	Case Workers, Specialist Teams, SC, Aunty, Mum, Previous Provider	Previous provider failed, crisis, local collaboration
Google	Research	Marketing Team, Website Team	Being found at time of search, brand recognition
Website	Consideration - Interest	Marketing Team, Website Team	Quality participant and house pictures, ease of enquiring (simple form)
Email (Company & Personal)	Enquiry - Next Steps	Senior Coordinator - Accommodation, SC, Mum	Immediate acknowledgement, speedy follow up, clear next steps. **BONUS**: Knew Aunty and her friend
Phone	Nurturing	Senior Coordinator - Accommodation, SC, Mum	Consistent communication and supportive team
House (Visit)	Nurturing	Senior Coordinator - Accommodation, SC, Mum,	Well presented, friendly and welcoming
Phone, Email	Conversion	Senior Coordinator - Accommodation, SC, Mum,	Feels confident in provider and decision to say yes
Word of Mouth, Reviews, Social Media	Advocacy	Happy Participants & Choosers, Support Coordinators, Referrers	Exceptional post-move support, perceived belonging, genuine care, ease of giving feedback, streamlined referral process

How Journey Mapping Improves Marketing

When you map the journey, you can:
- Tailor your messaging and resources to each stage
- Choose the right channels for the right people
- Track what's working and what's not (test and measure)
- Align your budget with your most valuable lead sources and conversion points
- Build trust through real stories, authentic visuals, and consistent follow-through

You move from 'spray and pray' to 'plan and perform'.

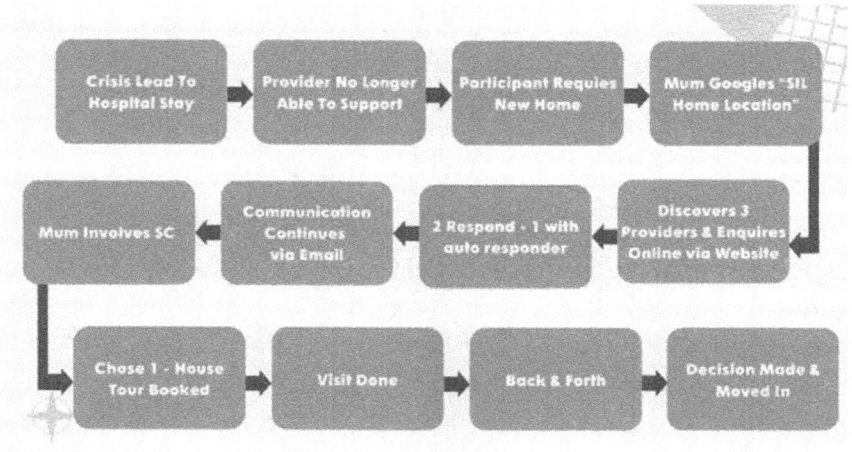

How Journey Mapping Improves Operations

This isn't just about marketing. This is where clarity over your Critical Client Flow makes the whole business better. (Credit to the fantastic work of David Jenyns in his book Systemology.)

You can:

- Create better systems for inquiry follow-up (set a standard response time, e.g. 6 to 12 hours, then have a process to email and SMS)
- Use CRMs like Monday.com, ActiveCampaign, HubSpot (or even a shared, secure online spreadsheet to start) to track enquiries from potential clients
- Set up automation to handle admin so your team can focus on relationships
- Get the sales and intake teams talking, so you know which leads are quality and why
- Train your frontline staff in client psychology, empathy, and a robust enquiry handling process

All this makes your business more consistent, more efficient, and more likely to succeed.

Digital Tools & Smart Tactics

I'm a big believer in using the tools we already have access to, especially when they give us real-world insight into what our audience wants and where we can show up better. For SIL providers, tools like **Google Keyword Planner, ChatGPT** and **LinkedIn Audience Insights** (and many others) play a huge role today. They give you data so you're not guessing, and that data can guide everything from your content calendar to your advertising strategy. Here are some examples below:

Using Google Keyword Planner to Prove Demand

One of the most practical things you can do is jump into Google Keyword Planner and check how many people are searching for what you offer. Let's say you have an SIL home in Hornsby. You find out there are 300 searches per month for 'SIL vacancy Hornsby'. That's real, bottom-of-the-funnel demand.

It tells you two things:

1. People are actively searching in your location.
2. You have an opportunity to get in front of them right when they're looking, especially if you aren't showing up organically.

This helps justify a local Google Ads campaign or gives you direction for your SEO strategy. It's not about throwing money at ads; it's about investing where the demand already exists.

LinkedIn Isn't Just for Job Seekers

LinkedIn is a seriously underused tool in this space. It's where your B2B audience (choosers) lives, such as support coordinators, OTs, case managers, and plan managers. You can build relationships, build trust, and build a reputation without spending a dollar (or you can invest in ads to speed this up).

If you're ready to go a step deeper, **LinkedIn Sales Navigator** lets you get super-targeted. You can search for support coordinators by job title, company, or location. This is how you size your market, build a referral pipeline, and reach the right people with the right message.

Even without paid ads, LinkedIn's **Ads Manager** can be used to explore the professional interests and demographics of your ideal referrers. It gives you real-time insight into who and how many of your prospects exist on LinkedIn.

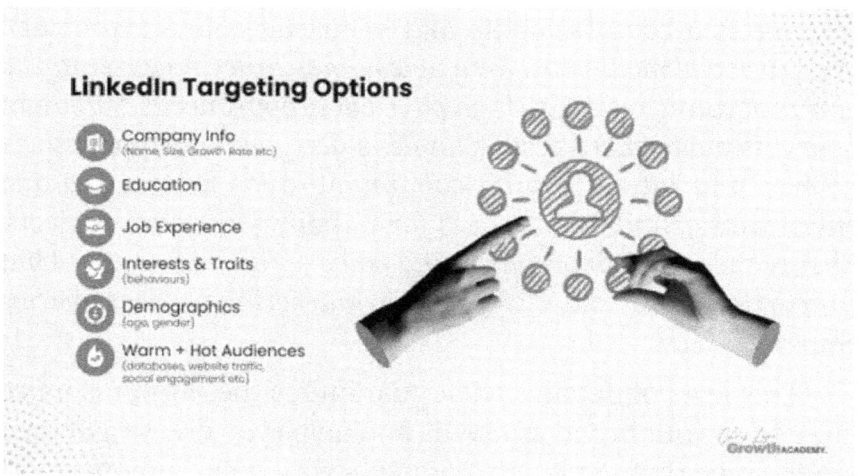

How AI Can Support Marketing (Without Losing the Human Touch)

AI isn't a magic solution, but it's a fantastic support act. I use it as a thought partner to help conduct research, ideate, draft, repurpose, and optimise. It saves time and removes the blank-page syndrome.

1. Tailored Approach and Keeping It Real
To avoid getting a generic response, think of it like this, your AI is a new team member, and you need to give it a proper job description and parameters to work with. In every conversation (or when building a custom agent), start with a prompt that provides a clear **role**, specific **instructions**, brand **tone**, **voice** and **constraints**, and as many **details** as possible.

For instance, instead of just asking for a social media post, you could prompt it this way:

Act as a compassionate and knowledgeable SIL provider. Write a social media post for a new home, targeting parents and carers of young men with high physical support needs. Highlight how this modern, accessible home is designed to support their hobbies and interests, with communal areas for gaming and entertaining, and quiet spaces for pursuing personal projects. Ensure the tone follows our brand voice of fun and youthful but supportive, and avoid using generic marketing phrases like 'we empower lives'.

This level of detail is what guarantees the output is more tailored to your brand, is useful, and helps you create a unique brand voice that genuinely connects with your audience.

2. Content Planning and Ideation

You don't need to guess what to post anymore. Start with your audience and the end in mind to get you started. You can prompt AI like this:

I'm a SIL provider in Perth supporting young males with high physical support needs. What are 10 common questions a parent might have when searching for an SIL home?

You can use the output to build blog topics, social media posts, or website content like FAQs or new service pages.

However, remember to always keep the 'human in the loop'. Never let AI work on its own in this sector. It's a co-pilot, not the pilot. Every piece of content, every drafted response, and every output should be reviewed and edited by a person. Your unique brand voice and values are your biggest asset. AI can't replicate your lived experience, your team's empathy, or the trust you've built in your community. Use it to do the heavy lifting of drafting, but make sure the final output has your fingerprints all over it.

3. Visual Planning Support

AI can even help you creatively brief your photo shoots and graphic designers, ensuring your brand's look and feel is consistent and authentic. Instead of relying on stock photos or generic designs, you can use AI to translate your brand's voice into a visual brief.

You can ask for concepts for a photoshoot like this:

Based on our post about 'creating a home that feels like family', what are five visual concepts we could capture in a team and participant photoshoot? We don't want it to look cliche or like the standard disability stock assets out there.

This leads to real, relatable visuals that are a true representation of the people you support, not another stock image of a person in a wheelchair that isn't representative of the people you support.

You can also use AI to brief a graphic designer. For example, you might ask:

We are launching a new community access program. What are three visual concepts for a social media graphic that communicate 'fun, community, and genuine connection'? Give me ideas for colours, imagery, and text layout that aren't generic.

This approach gives your creative partners a clear direction, ensuring they produce visuals that truly reflect your values and help your brand stand out.

Using AI to Improve Strategy, Not Just Content
You can also use AI to test and refine strategy. For example, feed it your competitors' home pages and ask:

What's their core message? How do they position themselves? What's the gap in the market?

This kind of basic audit can help you find your own point of difference and refine your messaging.

AI can also simulate buyer mindsets. You might prompt:

Imagine you're a support coordinator juggling 25 clients. What annoys you about SIL providers?

You'll uncover insights that can help you shape more empathetic messaging and service design.

Low-Cost Testing That Works

Testing your messaging doesn't need to be expensive. Here are a few low-cost or free ways to learn what your audience cares about:

Organic Methods
- Run polls on Instagram Stories or Facebook. For example: 'What's the hardest part of finding a new SIL home?'
- Test email subject lines and see which one gets more opens. That tells you what's resonating.
- Post two different versions of a caption or graphic and compare engagement.

Paid Methods
- Run two Facebook ads with different headlines or images. See which one gets the better click-through rate.
- Use Google Ads with different keyword match types or calls to action. You'll quickly see what's working based on cost per click.

It's not about being everywhere. It's about being in the right places with the right message at the right time.

Section 4: Sales Process & Promotion

Marketing only works if there's a sales process on the other end to catch the lead. Too often, I see great campaigns fail because no one followed up on the inquiries, or they took too long to respond. It's like turning on a tap but leaving the sink unplugged.

Here's what a basic but effective sales process should look like for any SIL business:

A Simple, Effective Sales Funnel for SIL

1. Lead Capture
This is when someone reaches out through a web form, phone call, direct email or social media message.

2. Initial Response
Whether automated or manual, send a message to acknowledge the inquiry and offer a calendar link or time to connect for quick follow-up.

3. Follow-Up Protocol
Have a documented system. How many times do you call? Do you follow up with SMS and email? Who's responsible? Use a CRM like HubSpot or ActiveCampaign. At minimum, a secure shared sheet is better than scribbled notes or forgotten inbox threads.

4. Meet & Greet
Make it easy to schedule and host this. All required documents should be digital and ready to go.

5. Data Capture and Internal Handover
Ensure all lead and participant information is captured properly and passed on to the right intake or care coordination team.

Clarity is key. Who owns which stage? What are the timeframes? Where is everything documented?

When Paid Advertising Works (and When It Doesn't)

Paid ads can be powerful, but they can also be a black hole if you're not ready. Here's my honest breakdown.

When It's Worth the Spend
- You've got a live vacancy and need quick traffic, BUT you must have great content, such as photos of a home (not an empty house), video tours, and a unique message about the type of home.
- You've validated that people are searching for terms like 'SIL vacancy Hornsby', and you aren't showing up organically.
- You've got a high-quality website with great storytelling and an inquiry process in place.
- You're ready to track results, test, and refine.

Google Ads are best for intent-driven searches.

Meta Ads (Facebook and Instagram) are great for storytelling and local awareness.

LinkedIn Ads are good for building B2B brand presence with support coordinators.

If you're using real stories and high-quality visuals, you're going to get better traction than you would with a stock image and a generic quote.

When It's a Waste of Money
- Your website is outdated or hard to navigate
- You're sending traffic to a general homepage with no call to action
- You don't have a defined follow-up process
- You haven't done your keyword or audience research
- Your SIL looks empty, soulless, and not like an inviting home
- When you don't have genuine stories to share

- If you are trying to be a nameless, faceless organisation with no human connection
- You expect ads to 'solve' your vacancy problems without any system to support them

Running ads without a solid plan is like trying to build a house without a blueprint. You'll spend money on materials and labour, but you'll have no idea where to put them.

The One Thing You Should Do This Month

If you do nothing else, do this, **humanise your brand**. Show your people. Share your story. Let people see who's behind the service.

Here's how:
- Create a system where support workers and managers can capture stories and get permission to share them
- Use real photos and videos of your homes and team
- Post about the little wins, not just the big milestones

That's what builds trust. And trust is what fills homes.

Bonus Tip: Stage your houses to look like a home. Don't advertise them with no furniture.

Section 5: Partnerships, Referrals & Ecosystems

In the NDIS world, relationships are everything. You can have the best home, the best staff, and the best systems, but if you're not known, trusted, and easy to work with, it makes things a lot harder, especially when it comes to referrals.

SIL providers often underestimate the power of their referral ecosystem. They rely on ads to bring in leads, when in fact, some of the highest-quality referrals come through business-to-business (B2B) relationships. These include support coordinators, allied health professionals, plan managers, and other providers who know your reputation and trust your team.

These people are the gatekeepers. If you're hard to deal with, unclear in your process, or slow to respond, you'll quietly be dropped from their mental shortlist.

Support Coordinators: Understand Their World

Support coordinators are busy. Many are carrying 25 to 50 clients and are under constant pressure to move things along. They don't have time for vague promises or chasing paperwork. They want providers who:

- Are clear about what they're offering
- Can communicate capacity and suitability quickly
- Follow through without hand-holding
- Genuinely care about outcomes

That means your messaging can't just be about what you offer; it has to clearly say who you support best, what your availability looks like, what the next step is, and who to contact. If you make their job easier, they'll keep coming back.

Build Your B2B Reputation on LinkedIn

These professionals spend time on LinkedIn, not to be sold to, but to connect, learn, and refer with confidence. A strong personal brand that shares value, insights, participant wins, and real stories can open doors that no cold email ever will.

You don't need to spend hours every day on it. Even once or twice a week, showing up with something useful or relatable makes you more visible and builds trust.

Be a 'Pleasure to Refer To'

That phrase comes up all the time in my conversations with coordinators. They'll say things like, 'They're just a pleasure to refer to.' That's your goal.

What does that look like in practice?

- Fast and respectful communication
- Clear eligibility criteria and information on who you help and who you don't
- Efficient onboarding steps
- Real relationships with real people
- Solutions when things get stuck

If you can do that consistently, you'll never have to ask for referrals; you'll earn them.

Think Like a Network Builder, Not Just a Provider

Get to know your local community. Host breakfast meetups. Offer to present at team meetings. Share updates on new services or vacancies, not in a needy or pushy way, but with the mindset of adding value.

Start mapping out your referral ecosystem:

- Who are the top 10 coordinators in your area?
- Which OTs, psychologists, or plan managers already trust you?
- Which hospitals or discharge teams could benefit from knowing your service?

Start there. Build with intention.

Messaging, Brand & Storytelling

Most providers don't have a marketing problem; they have a messaging problem. They don't know how to talk about themselves in a way that connects with the people they're trying to reach.

Too often, messaging is focused on the provider's needs, not the audience's reality. You see phrases like:

'We have a brand-new property in a great location.'
'We offer tailored supports.'
'We pride ourselves on quality.'

None of that stands out. None of it speaks to the actual fears, frustrations, or dreams of a parent trying to find a safe and loving home for their child or the support team around them.

The Most Powerful Messages are About Them, not You

The best messaging speaks to where the customer is right now, emotionally and practically. What are they worried about? What have they tried already? What haven't they been able to find?

Here's what good, targeted messaging can sound like:

- Do all other SIL Houses look like a waiting room? Ours has a dedicated gaming den and a patio that is actually used. We built this place for late-night debates and the kind of laughter you can hear down the street.
- Looking for an NDIS SIL home? Come visit us on a Tuesday, and see how your three new housemates value peace and quiet, learn to share a kitchen and build trust through baking.

- We're not 'choice and control'. We're a fully equipped woodworking shed, a mudroom for hiking gear, and a weekly gardening roster. This is the house for someone who wants to get their hands dirty, not just sit on a sofa.
- Stop battling to find the right NDIS SIL. When you call us, you get Sarah, our dedicated client support manager. She stays with you from the first email right through to your move-in date. A single person to make the hard parts simple.

That's how you connect. That's how you meet them where they are. That's how you stop the scroll.

The Power of Storytelling in a Trust-Based Sector

People don't buy into houses; they buy into the stories and dreams inside that home. Stories of transformation, stories of safety, and stories of people like them who found a place to thrive.

One of the most effective things you can do is share participants living their lives, whether big or small. Not for marketing fluff, but for human connection.

Example:

'When Josh moved in, he wasn't speaking much. Now, 12 months later, he's planning a group BBQ and asking to help with the cooking. It's the little things that show he feels at home.'

That's powerful. That's real. That's what families and support coordinators want to hear.

Don't Rely on Stock Images or Clichés

Your audience can tell when something is generic. They can feel when it's real. Ditch the overused phrases like 'person-centred', 'quality care', or 'tailored supports'. Instead, show it.

Use real photos. Show your team laughing with participants. Capture a shared meal, a walk in the park, or a moment of connection.

If you can't do that right now, plan a half-day content session or start with your team and what makes them truly qualified. Create a plan to gain permission from clients, capture moments, and start using visuals that reflect your service.

Build Your Brand as a Trusted Guide

Your brand isn't just your logo. It's how people feel when they interact with you. That feeling could be:

- Excited
- Reassuring
- Adventurous
- Human

Or whatever it is that truly creates a unique story for your brand.

If your website is filled with generic messaging, your emails are cold, or your ads are generic, that's the brand you're building, whether you mean to or not. Make sure everything, from your social posts and website to your inquiry form and phone calls, reinforces that you're the kind of provider they can trust to care for their loved one. BUT it must be unique to you!

Metrics, Data & Optimisation

If you're not tracking your numbers, you're just guessing. And in this sector, guessing is expensive. You could have the best-looking website, strong relationships, even good ads, but if you don't know what's actually working, you'll either overspend or miss key opportunities.

Data isn't about being technical, it's about being informed. You don't need to be a data analyst, but you do need to know your key numbers.

Know Your Funnel: From Lead to Move-In

Every NDIS business should be tracking the basic customer journey. For SIL, it can be simplified to look like this:

1. Website visit or social media discovery
2. Inquiry
3. Follow-up phone call or meeting
4. Tour or assessment
5. Move in

Each of these stages is a conversion point. You need to track:

- How many leads come in
- How many are qualified (tip: you must clearly define a definition of 'qualified' based on funding, housemate matching, if you can truly support, etc.)
- How many move to meet and greet
- How many become participants

When you start doing this, patterns emerge. You might realise that your website generates leads, but your follow-up is slow. Or your ads get clicks, but your inquiry form is confusing. Without data, these problems hide in plain sight.

Track Your Cost Per Lead and Lifetime Value

Here's a simple equation: if a new SIL client brings in $300,000 in revenue per year and stays with you for three years, what are you willing to pay to acquire that client? This number should be based on true profit, and if you don't know that, you need to start here. That's your ceiling.

Too many providers are flying blind, running ads without tracking cost per inquiry, cost per qualified lead, or having a true target cost per acquisition. You don't need complicated software to start. Even a basic spreadsheet or CRM can show trends.

Remember, not all inquiries are equal. You want quality over quantity. Data helps you see that clearly.

Simple Tools to Start with

- **Google Analytics:** track web traffic, bounce rate, and conversion goals.

- **Meta Business Manager:** review ad performance like cost per click and click-through rate, or cost per lead.
- **CRM (like HubSpot or ActiveCampaign, or a simple Google Sheet):** track lead stages, your follow-up process, qualified vs qualifies and number of interactions (touch points) required to 'convert'.
- **Heatmaps (e.g. Hotjar):** see how people interact with your website.

These tools give you the story behind the numbers. If people are dropping off your site after five seconds, you don't have a traffic problem; you have a messaging or design problem.

Listen to the Front Line Too

Your data isn't just numbers; it's also the feedback from your intake team. What are people saying on the phone? Are they confused, excited, overwhelmed?

Ask the person answering the phone: 'What are you hearing? What questions come up over and over?' or 'Where do people say they've heard about us?'

That qualitative data is gold. It tells you what to improve, what content to create, marketing channels to leverage or remove, and which objections to overcome before they even arise.

Long-Term Positioning & Growth

Filling one vacancy is great. Building a pipeline of consistent, high-quality leads who understand your values, trust your brand, and are ready to engage, that's how you future-proof your business.

Sustainable growth doesn't come from clever marketing campaigns alone; it comes from positioning yourself in the market as a trusted, values-led provider that delivers what they promise.

You must build a multi-channel approach that's equally driven by referrals and modern-day marketing.

Your Reputation is Your Growth Engine

In the NDIS space, word-of-mouth travels fast. If you're consistent, clear, and caring, people talk. Support coordinators talk. Families talk. If you're not, they talk even faster.

Your goal is to be the provider that people refer to without hesitation. That doesn't happen through a logo or ad; it happens when you build real relationships and back them with reliable systems.

Brand Building is a Long Game

Many providers focus all their energy on vacancy-based marketing. That's important. But brand marketing is what fills your vacancies faster and more consistently over time. Your brand is the sum of every interaction people have with your business.

That includes:
- The tone of your emails
- The content you and your team post online (and if you aren't, this should be a key starting point)
- The clarity of your website
- The speed of your response
- The look and feel of your tours
- The houses you decide to try and 'fill'
- The stories you tell publicly

Are you showing that you care? Are you helping people feel confident before they even contact you? Are you a truly values-led provider? Or did you simply react to 'opportunity' in the market, and find the first house you could that you yourself wouldn't live in?

Share Your Wins (and Lessons Too)

Don't be afraid to show your journey. Share the little wins, celebrations with participants, a team member's milestone, or something you've learned from a tough experience. This transparency builds trust and positions you as a real, human brand.

You can do this through:
- Social media stories

- A monthly email to your referral network
- Quick videos from your team
- Handwritten thank-you notes to referral partners

These small, consistent actions shape how people think and talk about your brand. Over time, that builds momentum.

Invest in Long-Term Relationships

It's not just about acquiring clients, it's about continuing the high-quality support and care you would want for your own family. Focus on the full experience from the first click to the first anniversary in the home and beyond. Make families feel involved. Give support coordinators updates they didn't even ask for.

That kind of care turns clients into advocates. It reduces churn. It increases referrals. It gives you more positive stories of change to share. It drives stable growth.

Final Thought: The Strategy of Deep Thinking

This chapter began with a simple idea: think before you act.

You've learned that frantically chasing leads when vacancies hit is not a marketing problem; it's a strategy problem, a failure to lay the groundwork when the boat wasn't leaking. We've replaced the generic 'we, we, we' problem with a powerful audience focus, anchoring every message in the functional and emotional reality of the people on the other end of the screen or reading the brochure. We've turned an empty house listing into an offer of a stable future, a unique experience, and a true place to call home.

The greatest campaigns, the most effective sales funnels, and the most reliable referral networks don't start with a budget; they start with clarity and deep thought about the person on the other end. This thinking begins when you stop viewing a vacancy as a revenue gap and start viewing it as an opportunity to provide a tailored, high-quality service. Your strategy isn't a complex document to be filed away; it's the daily, systematic application of that insight. From the words you use in a Facebook ad or on your website, to the professionalism of your intake process, to the competence of the support worker answering the door.

The Strategy-Execution Bridge

The path to a future-proof SIL business isn't found in a magic ad spend or a viral post. It's found in the simple, consistent discipline of putting the human being at the absolute centre of your strategy. This isn't just a philosophical approach; it's the most effective way to run your business. Deep thought about the client and their referral network gives you the data you need to be precise:

- When you understand the Support Coordinator's need for clear, rapid communication you know exactly what facts to emphasise on LinkedIn.

- When you understand the family's deepest fears about safety and community, you know the authentic stories and imagery that will stop the scroll on Facebook.

- When you understand the participant's needs for specific hobbies and interests, you know the niche phrases to use for Google Ads keyword targeting.

This combined approach of insight then execution is the work, and it is the only way to build a brand that not only survives the NDIS landscape but thrives in it.

The True Cost of Inaction

The question now isn't just, 'How do I fill my current vacancy?' The long-term, critical question you must carry forward is: 'Am I building a business that people will choose, or one they will simply tolerate?'

Tolerated providers rely on desperation. Chosen providers are built on trust.

Stop reacting. Start designing.

Design your message to solve the complex challenges of families, participants, support coordinators, and health professionals alike. Design your systems to make the journey effortlessly simple. Design your copy, visuals, and channels to ensure you are reaching the right people with a tailored, compelling message that proves you deliver what you promise.

Think before you act, and remember that for your end customer, choosing a home is the biggest decision of their life. So if you treat it that way, you will never run out of people who want to choose you.

CHAPTER 11

RETHINKING PARTICIPANT MATCHING WITH TECHNOLOGY

BY AARON COTTON

Aaron Cotton's journey into the world of disability housing wasn't planned. Originally a pharmacist, his path took an unexpected turn after a conversation with a friend opened his eyes to a broken system that he couldn't ignore. The more Aaron learned, the more it became clear: if his disability were more profound, his basic rights—like the right to choose who he lived with—would be taken away. That realization led him to a simple, yet powerful conclusion: this had to change. Aaron co-founded Marco Polo Portal, a platform designed to flip disability housing on its head and give people with disabilities the autonomy they deserve. He explains it like this: "You know how you get to choose who you live with? Well, often people with a disability don't. What we do is give that choice back."

Before Marco Polo, Aaron founded Acorn Homes, a Supported Independent Living provider that stood out for actually giving people control, not just paying lip service to empowerment. Aaron's work has earned him the Innovation Award at the Disability Leadership Institute and a place in Remarkable Tech's accelerator, but his true passion lies in creating real community impact. He's a straight-talker, driven by a desire to connect with others who are ready to reimagine the future of disability housing.

• • •

CONNECT WITH AARON AT:
WEBSITE: marcopoloportal.com
LINKED IN: @aaron-cotton

Author note: The opinions of this chapter are not entirely my own but the collective opinion of participants, families, providers, and even some government officials I have met whilst on my disability housing journey. Thank you to all the people who have shared their stories to help me write this chapter. In choice and good company, Aaron.

I'm not some tech-bro riding in like a medieval knight on a steed of self-righteousness, telling SIL providers they're doing it all wrong. SIL is the hardest support service under the NDIS. I'm a SIL provider myself. My service provision is located in Moreton Bay, Queensland. We have been operating for over five years, and it's been one of the hardest five years of my life. This is after I spent seven years as a pharmacist managing five regional stores. In my time, I have made what I like to call a massive number of mistakes and have found solutions to every one of them, but there are some key learnings I gathered along the way.

Supported Independent Living (SIL) has always promised more than it delivers. On paper, it's about freedom, dignity, and choice. In practice, it often looks like a game of Tetris—providers slotting people into whichever vacancy is open, regardless of whether it makes sense for the human being at the centre.

This is often not the provider's fault; it comes back to the debate about whether disability support businesses should even be allowed to make a profit or whether we revert to a charity model. It's harmful to the great work providers do when we sit in limbo between a free market and the shadow charity model of yesteryear.

This chapter isn't a policy brief or a how-to manual; it's a provocation. What if the way we approach participant matching in SIL isn't just outdated, but fundamentally broken? And what if technology, used thoughtfully, could give participants more control than ever before?

This isn't a utopian fantasy; it's already happening in pieces: in emerging new platforms, in innovative providers, in families refusing to accept 'good enough'. To get there, we need to unlearn habits, question assumptions, and take seriously the idea that who you live with shapes who you become.

In my experience, the heart of the issue is that participant matching has been treated as an afterthought. Providers tend to focus on property, compliance, and staffing logistics. The human dynamics of sharing a home—personalities, lifestyles, even small quirks—rarely make the checklist. If they do, they're rarely explored with the guidance of the participant or their family.

The system rewards occupancy rates, or rather, punishes vacancies. Funding structures incentivise providers to fill a bed quickly, not to fill it well. As long as the home is full and the books are balanced, we're on the right track ... wrong! The participant experience is often anything but balanced.

Time and time again, providers talk about wanting to 'secure and anchor a tenant'. On the surface, it looks smart for stability, but it's the single most dangerous thing you can do, especially when you've got a 1:3 participant setup. What you're really doing is planting a ticking time bomb in that home. You're also unknowingly creating a sense of entitlement for the participant who was placed first, because suddenly they feel as though the house is theirs alone. They stop having any incentive to welcome housemates because they already have the home to themselves. That's not matching—that's setting up future conflict.

Compatibility in SIL isn't just about whether people can co-exist without conflict. Too often, we assume that if people are the same age, gender, and share one common interest, they'll be best friends. Or conversely, if they don't tick those boxes, it simply won't work. It's about whether daily rhythms align enough to create a sense of comfort and safety. Shared values, communication styles, cultural background, even sleep habits all matter. In the 'abled world', flatmates negotiate these things before committing. The reality is very different in disability housing support.

In my own SIL business, some of the most unlikely pairings have turned out to be the best matches. Differences can either become pressure cookers if ignored or surprising strengths if embraced with openness and creativity.

When matching is done well, the difference is night and day. Take the story of Randy and Jen. On paper, they looked like the worst possible pairing: Randy, a 21-year-old guy who loved loud music and horror movies; and Jen, a 65-year-old woman who preferred sports and gardening. As a provider, we never would have put them together. But we let them decide.

It turned out that Randy had a deep affection for his grandparents, and Jen missed her grandkids. They built a bond around that connection, often sitting down together for tea and Tim Tams several times a week. Their home wasn't just a house; it became a hub of pride and connection. Complaints dropped to zero, staff turnover plummeted, and their quality of life improved dramatically. It was proof that the best matches aren't always the most obvious ones.

One of the key lessons I drew from being a service provider is that matching should never really be up to providers in the first place. Participants and their families are the ones who truly know what makes sense for their lives. Providers need to shift from being decision-makers and wannabe matchmakers to being facilitators—offering risk assessments, safeguards, and support, but not control.

Here's where the concept of Bike Shed Theory comes in. People correctly assume they can't build a nuclear power plant, but they incorrectly assume they can build a bike shed without much thought. Matching participants is treated like the bike shed—simple, easy, something anyone can do. In reality, it's more complex, nuanced, and high-stakes than most acknowledge. As Tim Ferriss explains in *The 4-Hour Body*, the easy-seeming problems often hide the deepest traps. The best outcomes happen when participants lead and providers respect that by stepping back.

You will often hear me say, "Providers will claim they embody choice and control, but it seems this is only true if it benefits them as the provider." The best providers, in my experience, are the ones doing the simple things well—giving real choice and control and empowering families and other stakeholders. Implement things like trial stays, detailed questionnaires, active involvement of families, and transparent communication. These providers don't just place people; they facilitate introductions and support participants in making informed choices.

When providers rush or rely solely on compliance, the risks multiply. A mismatched household is expensive, not just in dollars but in reputation. Staff leave because they're tired of constant conflict and management not acknowledging the issues occurring on the floor. Families talk to each other, and word spreads fast in this industry. Word of mouth will make or break you as a provider, registered or not.

We can all empathise with the provider that has a lynch mob after them as soon as they receive any form of bad press. No one wants to be that provider, so set up your systems correctly from the start to avoid pain in the future.

Let's look at this from the perspective of self-sufficiency.

When was the last time you made yourself a coffee and realised you were out of milk? Chances are, you simply hopped in your car and drove to the shop to buy more, or bought yourself a coffee in the Macca's drive-through. That's self-sufficiency—the ability to respond to your own needs without having to wait on anyone else. I am continually amazed by the feedback we get around this idea, because for many people living with disability, it isn't their reality. They can't head out when they need something. They're constantly reliant on others, even for the basics of life. When participants are finally given the opportunity to participate fully in their own lives, it's extraordinary the pride and accomplishment they feel from even small acts of independence. That kind of feedback is worth more than any compliance tick.

Better matching doesn't just improve participant lives; it improves provider sustainability. Stable houses mean lower staff turnover, fewer crises, and less reputational damage. Providers who invest in compatibility upfront save money over time and in the immediate term, rather than using the anchor tenant or vacancy-filling model. You, as an NDIS provider, will decide on the path forward.

The Future of Disability Housing

Looking ahead, there are two scenarios that I believe will play out.

The first is the widespread adoption of the ILO/ILA model. This model is built not out of provider-driven solutions but exhausted families looking for an alternative to mainstream housing options. ILO is based mostly on the premise of a 'host' family or individual providing informal care in return for a small stipend or payment to assist with the cost of living, for example, in the form of a rental subsidy.

On the surface, these approaches look fantastic, but there are major blind spots that aren't being discussed. In many ways, the model mirrors aspects of the child safety or foster care system, which is already struggling with a severe shortage of carers. There's also a significant risk of fraud, coercion, and harm when a single family or carer provides the lion's share of support. Without strong oversight and accountability, these situations can create the very conditions that led to tragedies like the case of Ann Marie Smith.

The second eventuality is more positive—as technology gets better and better, I anticipate we will see a complete shift to participant-dictated matching and housing within the SIL or shared model of support. With more SIL providers entering the market, choice is becoming increasingly real for participants, not just around who they live with, but also who supports them. To date, there are over 730,000 NDIS participants (50% are children), and there are over 210,000 providers (registered and unregistered). Let's say half of these providers deliver some form of in-home support; that's a six-to-one ratio. So what are you doing as a provider to stand out from the other providers?

The SIL vs ILO Debate

I see a common debate happening online regarding group homes and SIL. I want to get something straight—group homes are not SIL homes. However, many providers treat SIL like group homes and continue to implement institutional practices that SIL sought to abolish.

If SIL was treated as Supported 'Independent' Living, the debate would be over. Group homes should not be defined by the number of people living in them, although they often are; four or more people sharing is considered a group home. Group homes should be classified as any home that implements institutional practices over any number of disabled residents. I have visited many one-participant group homes, and ILO looks like a great option once you've witnessed one.

I also see an argument towards ILO rather than SIL. It's "I don't want to live with a bunch of strangers." I agree with this sentiment; living with people you don't know or choose is unacceptable. However, the Western world is facing a loneliness epidemic. As more people live alone, it leads to poorer physical and mental health outcomes.

You might say, "I'll live with my partner," and many people choose to live this way, but wasn't your partner once a stranger? Then you spent enough time with them to consider them your partner. Or have you known them since birth? Housemates, partners and friends all begin as strangers. It's up to each and every one of us to decide when a stranger becomes more than that.

Vanity Metrics

What's one thing providers can do to implement better SILs and not become a group home provider? Stop opening single-participant homes with 1:3 funding. It's a recipe for disaster for both you and the participant.

I see so many providers chasing growth for growth's sake. Too often, I see providers of all sizes (not just the smaller, newer ones) opening new unsustainable houses because they want to show off their vanity metrics - just for the ability to compete for status at the next conference or networking event.

If you have 20 homes but aren't making any profit because of an excessive number of vacancies, are you really more successful than the provider with five homes pulling in a tidy $800,000 profit each year?

A successful SIL house isn't the newest or flashiest; it's the one where participants feel safe, respected, and connected - much to the dismay of many SDA builders out there in the market.

I remember visiting two nursing homes in Broken Hill, New South Wales, that drove this point home. The first was brand new, beautifully designed, and filled with modern equipment and entertainment, yet it felt cold, with no life or soul. The second looked like an island of misfit furniture: poor lighting, broken items, even the main lounge TV didn't work. But the residents were laughing, chatting, and genuinely enjoying themselves. The culture was alive, and despite the circumstances, people were happier there than in the shiny new facility. In fact, residents were actively trying to move from the new facility to the older one.

Compatibility isn't a bonus; it's the foundation. Without it, even the best-intentioned providers fail.

The Viability of Trust

As an SIL provider, we kept asking ourselves why participants and their families didn't trust us. But when I draw on my experience as a foster carer and in trauma-informed care, I've realised the participants' ability to trust you often has nothing to do with you!

The participant experience looks a little something like this:

Grow up believing you're a burden on your family. This transitions to being a burden on society, perpetuated by the NDIS fraud narrative in mainstream media.

Be promised as an adult that you'll be looked after by a provider and the NDIS, only to learn later that you were seen as a $250,000 contract, not a human being.

Experience this a few times through churn.

Be subjected to higher levels of violence, abuse, and neglect.

Then be left to your own devices when your funding is exhausted by said providers.

Sounds pretty awful, doesn't it?

Poor matches leave scars that go far beyond household friction. Many people living with disability have also experienced trauma, so when a placement breaks down, it can feel like yet another relationship lost—another reminder that they're alone and excluded from what others call a "normal life."

Each failed match chips away at autonomy, confidence, and the fragile hope that home can be a safe and stable place. When you don't feel safe or respected in your own home, it compounds past trauma and reinforces the belief that the system doesn't really care.

How much trauma and trust would you have in "the system" after that kind of experience?

It's About the People, Not the Properties

A Biased Opinion on the Way Forward

If I could rewrite the rulebook on participant placements, page one would read in bold:

It's about the people, not the properties.

Every system, every process, and every decision should flow from that principle. When we forget it, we stop creating homes and end up with empty houses—and the cost of that mistake is paid in both dollars and dignity.

By now, you have probably grasped what I think the way forward looks like for Supported Independent Living. But this opinion isn't purely my own; it includes the 600 people at the time of writing who have signed up to Marco Polo Portal.

I would be lying if I told you that Marco Polo is a state-of-the-art technological innovation that incorporates the full potential of artificial intelligence, machine learning and quantum computing. Instead, it's built on some of the simplest technology out there. The primary difference is that the technology is implemented in a way that provides the tools for participants to find a housemate and a living situation that suits their needs. The beauty isn't in the technology itself, but in the correct implementation of technology.

It stops society from becoming the burden for people with disability, giving them the same human rights we all have–to live with people we choose. AI will find its way into the platform in the future, but it will only be implemented if it truly benefits both the participants and providers we're supporting.

"Okay, Aaron, that's great, but how is this different from any of the other vacancy-filling sites?"

I hate this question, but it's led me down a path of promoting brand awareness, which ultimately formed my decision to write this chapter.

All other platforms focus on the four walls participants live in. Marco Polo focuses on the individual and the power of grouping multiple individuals together of their own choosing.

We do this in two different ways:

1. **Provider grouping:** When a vacancy exists in a provider property, you advertise the *people* who currently reside in the property rather than the boring, empty room. You create a "group" and then invite other participants to join that group. This allows people to connect with people–not just property–and enables participants to choose who truly matches them, rather than leaving it up to the provider to decide (and often get wrong).

2. **Participant grouping:** This model is a little further from the norm. It works more like group dating. Participants or their coordinators sign up to the

platform, chat to one another, and create groups. Once they've found a group of people they vibe with, they can mark themselves as "ready for a provider." This is truly people-centric and enables providers to start new homes without the vacancy-filling model as their go-to. No excessive vacancy cost, and profitability from day one.

Rather than spell out why this is a better way of doing things, I'm going to show you two numbers:

- $507,326 – The net profit of my own small SIL provision using the principles outlined above.
- -$1,245,609 – The net loss of a large not-for-profit provider still implementing the group home model in the 2024–25 financial year.

Not-for-profit is right by definition and practice, but in a few years, they're more likely to be a not-in-existence provider.

Conclusion

Home is the foundation for any successful life. The NDIA has recognised that they want more people with disability in the community and in active work. This is impossible without having the right home as a foundation.

As an SIL provider, remember: you're creating that foundation in people's lives.

If you were to trade places with your participants tomorrow, would you be happy with what you've built?

CHAPTER 12
AI AND THE FUTURE OF TECH IN DISABILITY SUPPORT
BY SABEH HASSAN

Sabeh Hassan is the founder and CEO of Eriko AI, a company focused on practical applications of Artificial Intelligence.

With over 15 years of experience in consulting, government, and enterprise environments, he has led digital transformation initiatives and built scalable data platforms.

He also leads Sabeh Hassan Advisory, supporting organisations with AI strategy, digital transformation, and data-driven operating models. Sabeh is the co-creator of Auditly, an AI-powered compliance solution for NDIS and home care providers, helping services streamline documentation, reduce administrative load, and stay audit-ready while keeping care person-centred.

•••

CONNECT WITH SABEH AT:
WEBSITE: sabehhassan.com
EMAIL: sabeh@sabehhassan.com
LINKED IN: @sabeh-hassan

What AI Really Means for Disability Services

Artificial Intelligence still feels abstract to many people working in disability services. It often sounds like something made for big tech companies, not for day-to-day care. But AI is already being used in frontline support. For Supported Independent Living providers, its relevance is immediate.

At its core, AI is a system that helps reduce repetitive thinking tasks. It handles routine or time-consuming work so staff can focus on the human side of their roles. That might mean help with documentation, scheduling, or identifying patterns in participant behaviour. AI doesn't replace people, it gives them more space to do the work only people can do.

This is important because teams are under pressure. Admin tasks have increased. Documentation needs to be more detailed. Providers are constantly managing compliance, audits, and risk. Most of this is done manually across disconnected systems. The result is burnout, staff turnover, and inconsistent service delivery. AI gives us a way to remove some of that pressure while maintaining or improving quality.

These tools already exist. Communication apps like Voiceitt or Proloquo2Go help non-verbal participants communicate clearly. Wearables can alert staff when a fall occurs or when behaviour changes. Home automation can be adapted so that a person can control their environment through voice or motion. These are not future innovations; they're in use today, with participants who are seeing real benefits.

There are also AI systems that help providers spot early signs of concern. By looking at data like sleep, movement, or mood patterns, they can highlight when something is changing. This can prompt early intervention, whether that means a medication review, a care plan update, or a conversation with the participant and their support network. These tools are designed to support safety, not replace judgement.

For providers, the most practical value is often behind the scenes. Some teams are already using AI to write draft progress notes, identify gaps in shift coverage, and spot billing anomalies. These systems work quietly in the background, improving speed and accuracy. They're not expensive, and they don't require a full digital overhaul to get started.

The key is to be deliberate. Small providers don't need complex platforms; they need tools that solve specific problems and fit into their existing systems. That might start with one documentation tool that saves an hour per day. Over time, those gains add up.

AI isn't a vision for the future; it's part of the present. The challenge is making sure it's used to support people, not replace them. When done well, it creates space for deeper connection and better outcomes. That's the opportunity in front of us now.

Saving Time Without Cutting Corners

In most SIL businesses, the day never ends with everything done. Staff are writing notes late at night, compliance tasks pile up, and rostering becomes a spreadsheet jigsaw puzzle. The operational side of support is where time disappears, and it's also where technology can have the biggest impact.

Providers using AI-enabled documentation tools are cutting their progress note time by half. Rostering platforms with automation features are reducing admin time by more than 60%. These are not promises from tech vendors; they're results from providers using the tools correctly.

One provider we worked with was rostering manually across four houses. It took two staff members almost a full day each week to manage changes, fill shifts, and balance availability with participant preferences. After switching to an AI-supported rostering tool, that task now takes under two hours. More importantly, the team is no longer firefighting; they're planning.

Documentation is another pressure point. Many support workers feel they spend more time writing about support than delivering it. AI-assisted note generation can help here, especially when it's integrated into the workflow. Staff can speak into a device, and the tool generates a structured draft note that meets compliance standards. The worker then reviews it, adds their context, and submits. It doesn't remove responsibility, but it makes the process faster and more consistent.

These kinds of tools also reduce duplication. When rostering systems talk to payroll, and documentation connects with compliance reporting, tasks aren't repeated across three platforms. That means less friction. It also means fewer errors and fewer things falling through the cracks.

One of the most overlooked benefits is decision support. AI can assist managers by flagging when a staff member is overworked, when shift patterns don't align with support plans, or when documentation is missing key elements. These alerts allow teams to act early, instead of reacting after something goes wrong.

The concern some people have is that automation will compromise quality, but we have seen the opposite. When staff aren't overloaded with repetitive admin, they can spend more time engaging with participants. That improves consistency, which supports better outcomes. It also helps with retention. People are more likely to stay when they feel their time is being used well.

Technology shouldn't get in the way; it should support the work. When it's set up to do that, the results are immediate. Better planning. Fewer mistakes. More time for people.

Predictive, Not Reactive

The next big shift is moving from responding after incidents to preventing them in the first place. Much of the NDIS system is built around response. An incident happens, a report is written, a review takes place, and a plan is updated. But by the time all of that happens, the damage is already done. The focus now needs to shift from responding to preventing. That is where AI has real potential.

The goal is to identify risk early, before it becomes a problem. Not through guesswork, but through data that is already being collected. When patterns are tracked over time, across behaviour, sleep, movement and engagement, early changes become visible. It becomes possible to see warning signs. And when those signs are flagged automatically, staff can act sooner.

This is already happening with some wearable devices. Sensors can track movement and alert staff when someone has been in the same position too long, which might indicate a fall or a medical issue. Others detect changes in walking patterns or posture that could signal a decline in mobility. These alerts can be real-time to support staff, even if they are not in the room.

There are also behavioural tracking systems that monitor signs of agitation or distress based on voice tone, movement, or facial cues. When used respectfully and with consent, they can help reduce escalation. Staff are notified before a situation becomes unsafe, and that allows them to step in with the right kind of support.

Medication adherence is another area where predictive tools are starting to make a difference. Smart systems can flag missed doses or irregular schedules, and prompt follow-up before health issues arise. The same applies to nutrition, hydration, and sleep monitoring. When these areas are tracked properly, staff can focus less on paperwork and more on meaningful intervention.

None of this replaces human oversight. The technology is there to support better timing and better decisions. The aim is not to take control away from staff or participants. The aim is to reduce harm and improve stability.

This kind of early-warning approach also benefits families. Instead of finding out after an incident has occurred, they receive reassurance that the right systems are in place to avoid problems in the first place. That builds trust and confidence, which are often missing when families feel left out or uninformed.

The long-term effect is that homes become calmer. Staff are less reactive. Participants feel safer. And providers spend less time on reports and investigations. That is not just about efficiency. It is about quality of life.

Moving from reactive to proactive support takes time. It requires planning, clear protocols, and a culture that sees technology as a support tool, not a surveillance system. But when it is done well, the shift is significant. Preventing risk is always better than responding to it.

Sabeh Hassan

Addressing Fear and Ethics

Technology in disability support isn't neutral. The way it's introduced, used, and explained carries consequences. For every provider who's excited about new tools, there's another who's cautious or concerned. These concerns aren't just emotional responses; they're grounded in real risks that need to be taken seriously.

One of the most common fears is job loss. When people hear that AI can automate parts of documentation, rostering, or incident detection, they assume it will reduce the need for staff. In reality, the opposite is happening. The sector continues to face workforce shortages, and no software can replace the trust, empathy, or decision-making that frontline workers provide. What AI can do is remove the busy work that distracts people from those core responsibilities. It creates space, not cuts.

Another fear is that technology will depersonalise care. If too much focus is placed on data or automation, there's a risk of reducing individuals to risk profiles or behaviour summaries. That's where ethical design matters. Technology should support better connection, not distance. It should highlight where support is needed, not act as a substitute for human presence.

Privacy is also a real concern. When devices are collecting information, participants and families need to know what's being recorded, who can see it, and how it will be used. That includes things like audio monitoring, movement tracking, and digital documentation. Transparency isn't optional. If you can't explain how a system works or what decisions it's making, you shouldn't be using it.

Consent must be at the centre of all technology use. That means clear, accessible information for participants and families, and real opportunities to opt in or out. It also means building feedback loops into the system. If something feels intrusive or uncomfortable, people need a way to raise that, and providers need to listen.

There's also the issue of bias. AI systems are trained on data, and if that data reflects inequality or misrepresentation, the outcomes will carry that same bias. For example, a predictive system might flag certain behaviours as high-risk based on patterns that don't apply to every individual or cultural background. If those systems aren't audited and tested properly, they can reinforce discrimination instead of improving support.

This is why human oversight is non-negotiable. AI should never operate in isolation. Every decision or alert it generates needs to be reviewed and understood by a person who has context. That's what the sector means by human-in-the-loop. The technology supports the process, but it doesn't take over. Providers remain accountable for outcomes.

We also need to be realistic about capability. Not every provider has the resources to implement complex systems or manage the risks that come with them. That's why simplicity and clarity matter. If a tool is too hard to understand or too expensive to maintain, it won't deliver the value it promises.

Ethical use of AI isn't just about ticking boxes; it's about building trust over time. That trust is earned when people see that technology is being used to improve their experience, not replace it. It's reinforced when participants are involved in decisions and when feedback shapes the system over time.

Done well, AI can support care that's more consistent, more responsive, and more personalised, but it must always remain grounded in the values of the sector. Human rights, dignity, choice, and inclusion can't be outsourced. They have to stay at the centre of everything.

Ethics in Practice (quick checks)

- **Consent and transparency:** plain-language notices, opt-in/out recorded.
- **Data minimisation:** collect only what you use, set retention periods.
- **Bias testing:** review alerts across different cohorts and cultures.
- **Human-in-the-loop:** define who reviews each class of alert.
- **Audit trail:** log who accessed what, when, and why.

First Steps for SIL Providers

For most SIL providers, the idea of implementing AI sounds out of reach. It brings to mind expensive systems, technical complexity, and the fear of making the wrong choice. But the reality is much simpler. You don't need to overhaul your business to start using smarter tools. You just need to start with a real problem.

How to Start (four steps)

1. **Pick one problem** (e.g. progress notes taking 2+ hours/day).
2. **Involve staff early** (map the 'current way' and pain points).
3. **Pilot one tool** in one house/team for 2–4 weeks.

4. **Measure, then scale** (time saved percentage, error rates, staff feedback, participant impact).

The most common entry point is documentation. Progress notes, shift reports, and incident records take up significant time. That time is often unstructured, inconsistent, or duplicated across platforms. AI-assisted tools can support staff by generating draft notes from spoken input, structured forms, or even basic templates. These tools don't remove the need for review or compliance; they help reduce the blank-page problem that slows people down.

Another simple starting point is rostering. Many providers still manage rosters with spreadsheets or basic scheduling software. This creates gaps, errors, and a heavy reliance on manual coordination. Smarter rostering platforms can recommend shifts based on staff qualifications, availability, and participant needs. They can also help flag when someone is at risk of being overworked or when a service agreement requires adjustment.

These tools are already available. They don't require custom development. In many cases, they integrate with the systems that providers are already using. The challenge isn't finding the technology, it's knowing what to prioritise. That's why the most effective approach is to focus on one clear issue at a time. Choose a problem that creates regular friction. Test one tool that addresses it. Measure the results. If it works, expand. If it doesn't, adjust. The goal isn't digital transformation. The goal is progress that can be sustained.

The other key is involving your team. If you choose tools without staff input, you risk low adoption. If you ask for feedback early, people will tell you where the pain points are and how they currently work around them. That insight is essential for choosing tools that will be used.

Cost is another consideration, but it's important to look at cost in relation to time saved, errors avoided, and staff retention. A well-chosen system doesn't need to be large or complex to make a meaningful difference; it just needs to solve a real problem in a way your team understands.

The first step isn't technical; it's cultural. Be curious, ask questions, and don't try to solve everything at once. Start with something simple, make it better, and grow from there.

Foundations Before Features

The biggest risk in adopting technology isn't that it fails, it's that it's never used. Many providers invest in tools that look impressive on paper but fail to deliver value in practice. This usually happens because the focus was on features, not foundations.

A provider might buy a sophisticated platform with automation, dashboards, and integration options. But if the team does not understand how to use it, or if there's no process to maintain it, the tool becomes shelfware. It sits in the background while staff go back to their spreadsheets and emails. That's why digital maturity matters more than digital ambition. Before any provider looks at advanced systems, they need to be confident that the basics are in place. That includes things like reliable internet in homes, secure devices for staff, consistent use of existing software, and clear processes for communication and data entry.

It also means knowing your data. If your records are inconsistent, incomplete, or stored across multiple systems, no AI tool will give you meaningful insights. The quality of the output depends entirely on the quality of the input. That includes progress notes, incident reports, rostering logs, and participant preferences. Cleaning that data and putting good habits in place is more valuable than chasing new software.

Culture is another key factor. If people in the organisation see technology as a threat or a burden, they'll resist it. That's why leadership matters. Providers need to communicate why changes are happening, what the expected benefits are, and how staff will be supported. This isn't just about training, it's about trust.

We often talk about digital transformation like it's a software rollout, but real transformation happens when people think and work differently. That takes time, and it takes reinforcement. One-time training isn't enough. There needs to be support, feedback loops, and space for people to make mistakes while learning.

Another common pitfall is trying to implement too many systems at once. A provider might invest in a rostering tool, a CRM, a documentation system, and a reporting dashboard, all in the same quarter. The result is confusion. People don't know where to look or what to prioritise. Integrations fail. Support requests spike. Eventually, the organisation pulls back and reverts to old habits.

A better approach is to build one layer at a time. Start with the core systems. Make sure they're stable, understood, and consistently used. Then look at what can be added on top to support that foundation. This reduces risk and makes it easier to measure progress.

It's also important to review what you already have. Many providers are sitting on underused features in their current systems. Rather than adding new platforms, it might make more sense to optimise what's already in place. That could mean automating a workflow, activating a reporting function, or setting up notifications for missing documentation.

Finally, make sure someone owns the system. Too often, technology is introduced with no clear responsibility for managing it. That leads to drift. If no one is checking usage, updating processes, or listening to feedback, the system becomes static. Assigning ownership, whether to a staff member, team, or external partner, helps ensure the technology continues to evolve with the organisation.

Technology doesn't create strategy; it supports it. That's why strong foundations matter. When the basics are right, even simple tools can make a big difference. When the foundations are weak, even the most advanced systems will fall short.

Keeping Technology Person-Centred

For all the focus on systems and tools, the purpose of technology in disability support should never change, it exists to improve people's lives. That means it must always stay connected to the human experience.

The best use of AI isn't the most advanced; it's the one that supports independence, dignity, and connection. In the future, the most effective systems won't be the ones with the most features; they'll be the ones that feel invisible. Technology will run in the background, adjusting to needs without getting in the way. That is the goal, to design supports that respond to people, not make people adjust to the system.

We're already seeing the first signs of this. Environments that adapt lighting or noise levels to reduce sensory overload. Devices that help participants communicate more easily, without needing constant staff assistance. Systems that learn from routines and suggest improvements without replacing human decision-making.

But staying person-centred doesn't happen by default; it requires ongoing work. Providers need to ask: 'Who is this tool helping? Is it making things easier for the person receiving support, or just for the people delivering it?' Both matter, but the person at the centre needs to remain the priority.

That's why co-design is essential. The people using the support, participants, families, support workers, need to be part of the conversation when technology is introduced. Their feedback should shape how systems are chosen, how they're configured, and how they're improved over time.

This also means providers need to be careful about what they measure. Quality isn't the same as quantity. Data must be used with purpose.

In the long term, the providers who succeed with technology won't be the ones who adopt it the fastest; they'll be the ones who stay clear on why they're using it, who they're serving, and how they measure value.

Technology will continue to change. It will become faster, cheaper, and more powerful. But the need for connection, for trust, and for real human care will remain. The future isn't about choosing between people and systems; it's about making sure the systems we choose serve the people first. The best technology disappears into the background, leaving the person at the centre.

Leading Through Change

Adopting new technology isn't just a technical shift; it's a leadership decision. Whether you're running a small SIL service or managing a growing team across multiple sites, your mindset will shape how technology is introduced, how it's received, and whether it makes a difference.

The providers that lead the next phase of the sector aren't necessarily the ones with the biggest budgets or the most advanced software; they're the ones who are willing to think clearly, ask good questions, and build systems around the people who use them. That includes participants, families, support workers, and administrative teams.

This kind of leadership isn't reactive; it's intentional. It starts with understanding what problems you're solving, not what products you're buying. It means taking time to test tools properly, listening to staff feedback, and making decisions based on long-term fit rather than short-term excitement.

It also means being honest about where your organisation is now. If your systems are still heavily manual, start by getting the basics right. If your team lacks confidence with digital tools, build digital literacy before introducing new platforms. If your data is disorganised, fix that first. These steps aren't flashy, but they're essential.

The most dangerous thing you can do is follow hype without a plan. There's no shortcut to sustainable change. But there is a pathway, and it's made up of small, practical moves. One tool that works well. One process that improves staff time. One system that helps reduce risk. When those improvements are built on strong foundations, they compound.

Being a technology-informed provider doesn't mean turning into a tech company; it means becoming an organisation that understands where value comes from and how to deliver it consistently. It means using tools to support the people at the centre of your work, not just to meet compliance or tick boxes, but to deliver care that is more responsive, more respectful, and more sustainable.

There's still a lot of noise in the space. More platforms. More solutions. More promises. It's easy to feel like you're behind or not doing enough. But the providers who succeed in the next phase of the NDIS won't be the fastest adopters; they'll be the ones who build carefully, keep people involved, and measure progress in outcomes, not just features.

Technology isn't going away. The question is whether we'll use it thoughtfully or reactively. As a provider, you have a choice, you can wait and be forced to adapt when pressure mounts, or you can lead, starting with simple, clear steps that support your team and your participants.

The opportunity is real. So is the responsibility. Use both wisely.

CONCLUSION: KEEP GOING, KEEP BUILDING

BY TANIA GOMEZ

If there's one thing this book makes clear, it's this, good SIL doesn't happen by accident, it's built with intention, structure, and a deep understanding of what's at stake.

Running an SIL service means you're holding a lot at once: people, property, rosters, claims, safety, compliance, and the well-being of those you support. Every decision you make has a ripple effect. There's no room to guess. No space for shortcuts. But there's also no one-size-fits-all playbook.

That's why this book exists.

Each chapter came from people living and breathing the work: providers, auditors, clinicians, team leaders, and innovators who've taken what they've learned and shared it here without ego or filter. They've spoken honestly about what works, what doesn't, and what they're still figuring out.

To every contributor, thank you. Your insight is what lifts this from being just another resource to something real, practical, and worth returning to.

And to you, the reader, thank you for making the time. For choosing to do this work with care. Whether you're just starting or you've been in the sector for years, the fact that you're still showing up to learn says everything about the kind of provider you are.

WHAT NOW?

Start small. You don't need to overhaul everything at once. Begin by choosing one action from the chapters below and putting it into practice in your service:

Part 1: Home is Where the Heart is

Scott Chapman, Healthy Homes
Walk through one of your homes as if you were a new resident moving in tomorrow. What needs to change for it to feel safe, clean, and welcoming?

Caroline Yates, Getting Complex Care Right
Review your current complex care participants. Is your clinical oversight documented and active? What are your biggest risks right now?

Luke Wilson, Meeting the Participant Where They're At
Choose one participant and check, is their SIL support plan still relevant to their current goals and preferences? If not, update it.

Ryan Simmon, What Good Supports Feel Like
Ask three participants, 'What makes you feel safe and respected in your home?' Let their answers guide a team conversation about support quality.

Part 2: The Pulse of the Practice

Dave Wells, Building Strong Frontline Leadership
Identify one team leader and ask them what support they wish they had. Build a basic structure to help them lead with more clarity and confidence.

Josh Pix, Claiming and Its Impact on the Bottom Line
Run a quick audit of your SIL claiming. Are you getting paid for every hour of service delivered? If not, dig into why and fix it at the source.

Charlene Woodbine, Building Teams that Stay
Look at your last three staff exits. What were the real reasons they left? What would it take to keep your next three hires long-term?

Tania Gomez, Setting a Strong Foundation with Quality Processes
Choose one quality process, maybe incident reporting or onboarding, and tighten it. Make it clear, repeatable, and documented.

Part 3: Reimagining Independent Futures

Dr Heena Sinha, Using Technology to Optimise Workflows
Map one key workflow (for example, onboarding or rostering) and identify one step that can be automated, simplified, or removed.

Chris Lapa, Think Before You Act
Before launching a new site or service, ask yourself: 'Why now, and what problem are we solving?' Create a checklist for decision-making.

Aaron Cotton, Rethinking Participant Matching with Technology
Review one recent participant placement. Was it a good match? Why or why not? What data could have helped you make a better decision?

Sabeh Hassan, AI and the Future of Tech in Disability Support
Pick one area in your service that creates daily friction (like rostering, documentation, or scheduling) and research one tech tool to test.

KEEP LEARNING WITH US

If this book has sparked something, don't stop here. You're not alone in trying to build something better; there's a whole community of providers across the country navigating the same challenges and asking the same hard questions.

The best SIL providers I've worked with have one thing in common, they don't isolate. They stay connected, they keep learning, and they surround themselves with people who push them to grow. If that sounds like something you need, here's where to start:

The SILosophy Podcast

This is where the real talk happens. Each episode is a conversation with someone inside the SIL space: providers, team leaders, clinicians, disruptors, all sharing what's working, what's not, and what needs to change. It's practical, raw, and refreshingly honest.

The SIL Summit

Our flagship event series. These are full-day, in-person experiences where we bring the sector together to focus on what actually matters. You'll hear from keynote speakers, participate in panel sessions, and meet other providers who are just as committed to doing this well. If you want to be part of the movement to lift the standard of SIL in Australia, this is where that conversation is happening.

The Provider Collective

Our free online community for NDIS providers is built to educate, support, and connect. You'll find resource libraries, live masterclasses, expert Q&As, downloadable templates, and a growing community of people who genuinely want to improve their practice. It's the ongoing support many providers have been missing.

Reach Out to the Authors

Every contributor to this book brought something real, not just theory, but experience. Many of them are active in the sector, running services, consulting, leading teams, or advocating for change. If someone's chapter resonated with you, reach out. Ask questions. Start a conversation. These are people who care deeply about this work, and you might be surprised how willing they are to connect, collaborate, and keep building together.

Work with Me One-on-One

If you're feeling stuck, overwhelmed, or just unsure where to start, book a free 15-minute consult. Whether it's audit readiness, quality systems, or just getting your head around what's going wrong, I'm here to help. You can book directly through my website or reach out to me on social media.

This work is complex, and there's no perfect roadmap, but there are people walking the path with you. Let's keep learning. Let's keep building. Let's keep showing up together.

WE'RE BETTER TOGETHER

This work is heavy. You're not imagining that. The responsibility that comes with running SIL services is immense. You're shaping people's homes, their safety, their sense of dignity, and their day-to-day quality of life.

It's complex, often thankless, and there's rarely time to pause and reflect, let alone ask for help. But you don't have to carry it all on your own.

If this book has reminded you of anything, I hope it's this, the sector is full of good people. People who care. People who are in it for the right reasons. People who don't have all the answers but are willing to keep showing up anyway. That's where the change starts with providers who lead with integrity and keep learning in the middle of the mess.

So keep going. Reach out when something lands. Tell someone what helped. Share the wins and the lessons. Ask better questions. Open up the conversations no one else is having. Because when we stop pretending to have it all figured out, we create space to figure it out together.

The sector doesn't need more perfect policies or polished marketing; it needs more honest conversations, smarter systems, and consistent action from people who give a damn.

That's you.

Let's build a sector where participant voice matters more than paperwork. Where frontline workers feel supported, not stretched. Where providers back each other instead of competing for scraps. And where we raise the standard not because someone told us to, but because it's the right thing to do.

Because when SIL works well, lives change. And that's always worth fighting for.

Tania Gomez

OTHER BOOKS BY TANIA GOMEZ
& INDUSTRY LEADERS

www.ingramcontent.com/pod-product-compliance
Lightning Source LLC
Chambersburg PA
CBHW031149020426
42333CB00013B/577